SPAIN'S SENDERO HISTÓRICO:
THE GR1

About the Author

John Hayes is a retired management consultant with degrees from Liverpool University and University College London. Immediately after finishing work in 2011 he embarked on an epic 5000km trek across Europe, walking from Tarifa in Spain to Budapest. The veteran of long treks in the Alps, Spain and the Himalayas, John has written for numerous walking and trekking magazines. John first walked the GR1 in early 2013 and has made two return trips.

When exploring new routes in Spain, John enjoys the advice and support of Juan Holgado, whose website JuanHolgado.com is one of best-known local sources on Spanish walking.

SPAIN'S SENDERO HISTÓRICO: THE GR1

by John Hayes

CICERONE

2 POLICE SQUARE, MILNTHORPE, CUMBRIA LA7 7PY
www.cicerone.co.uk

© John Hayes 2015
First edition 2015
ISBN: 978 1 85284 569 8

Printed by KHL Printing, Singapore
A catalogue record for this book is available from the British Library.
All photographs are by the author unless otherwise stated.

Route mapping by Lovell Johns www.lovelljohns.com
Contains OpenStreetMap.org data © OpenStreetMap
contributors, CC-BY-SA. NASA relief data courtesy of ESRI

Updates to this Guide

While every effort is made by our authors to ensure the accuracy of guidebooks as they go to print, changes can occur during the lifetime of an edition. Any updates that we know of for this guide will be on the Cicerone website (www.cicerone.co.uk/569/updates), so please check before planning your trip. We also advise that you check information about such things as transport, accommodation and shops locally. Even rights of way can be altered over time.

The route maps in this guide are derived from publicly-available data, databases and crowd-sourced data. As such they have not been through the detailed checking procedures that would generally be applied to a published map from an official mapping agency, although naturally we have reviewed them closely in the light of local knowledge as part of the preparation of this guide.

We are always grateful for information about any discrepancies between a guidebook and the facts on the ground, sent by email to info@cicerone.co.uk or by post to Cicerone, 2 Police Square, Milnthorpe LA7 7PY, United Kingdom.

Front cover: The Pyrenees – the backdrop to the GR1

CONTENTS

Symbols used on route maps

	route
	alternative route
(S)	start point
(F)	finish point
(SF)	start/finish point
	glacier
	woodland
	urban areas
	regional border
	international border
	station/railway
▲	peak
⬤ ◯ ◯	town/village/abandoned village
⬆ ⬘	manned/unmanned refuge
⌇	campsite
■	building
⬤ ■ †	church/monastery/cross
✳	viewpoint
⟩⟨	pass
·	water feature
⬔	castle

Relief
in metres

3000–3200	
2800–3000	
2600–2800	
2400–2600	
2200–2400	
2000–2200	
1800–2000	
1600–1800	
1400–1600	
1200–1400	
1000–1200	
800–1000	
600–800	
400–600	
200–400	
0–200	

SCALE: 1:100,000

0 kilometres 1 2

0 miles 1

Contour lines are drawn at 50m intervals and highlighted at 200m intervals.

GPX files

GPX files for all routes can be downloaded for free at www.cicerone.co.uk/member.

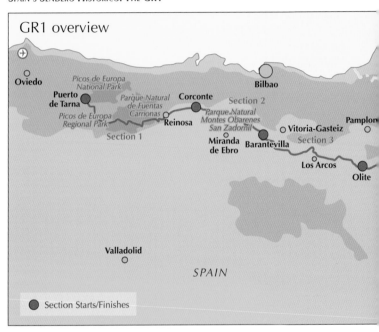

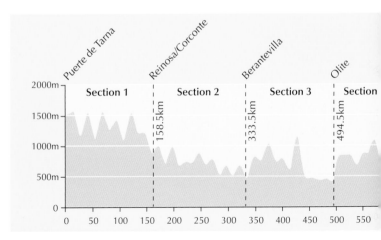

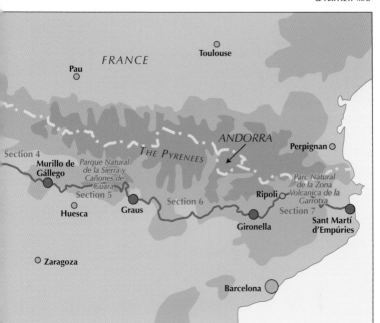

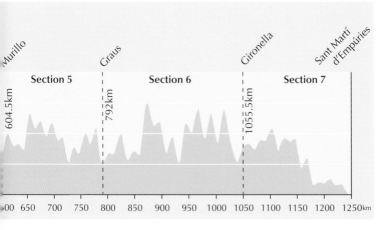

Approaching Noguera-Ribagorçana (Section 6, Stage 3) in the Sierra del Montsec

INTRODUCTION

The Pyrenees from Lluçà (Section 7, Stage 1)

The Sendero Histórico (or GR1) is a trail that combines great scenery with a gentle lesson in Spain's fascinating history. Spain has an impressive selection of long-distance paths and experienced Spanish walkers would tell you that this is the best of them – little known outside Spain as it may be.

Traversing the north of Spain it sits in the shadow of world's most famous walk, the Way of Saint James (the 'Camino di Santiago'), and offers a completely different experience. The 'Camino' had one aim: to get pilgrims to Santiago de Compostela as quickly as possible. It's a sort of medieval motorway. The GR1, on the other hand, is a relatively modern invention and it's in no rush. There is nothing direct about this route. Designed for walkers, it meanders through some of the best scenery northern Spain has to offer and, at the same time, visits key locations in the development of modern Spain.

Walking in Spain is a special experience. Spain was the last country in Western Europe to experience rural depopulation, and the remnants of an ancient infrastructure where everyone walked are still there. The GR1 follows paths and trails that, until the 1960s, were the main way people and their animals moved from

11

Peña Espigüete from the Collado de Cruz Armada in the early stages of the trek (Section 1, Stage 3)

village to village. Although, sadly, the days when every village had a bar, cantina or hostal have now gone, there are still just enough to make walking from place to place the best way to travel.

Travelling from west to east across Spain, the Sendero starts at the Puerto de Tarna, a pass on the regional border between the Asturias and Castilla y León, heads east along the southern flank of the Cantabrian Mountains, the plain of Navarre and the foothills of the Pyrenees ('Prepirinio' in Spanish) and then finishes on the Mediterranean coast at Sant Martí d'Empúries near L'Escala. Although it's a long walk, some 1250km, and mountainous, involving over 39,000m of climb, it's not difficult. If

you're reasonably fit, the only thing you need to enjoy it is time.

The route crosses six Spanish 'Autonomous Regions' – the components of what is a very federal country. The original idea was to establish a coast-to-coast walk from the Atlantic to the Mediterranean, but the first two regions on the route – Asturias and Galicia – didn't buy into the vision hence the Puerto de Tarna start. For those walkers who want to dip their toes in both oceans this guide describes how to extend the route to Finisterre and the Atlantic using other GR routes (see Appendix B).

An important feature of mountain walking in Spain, unlike much of Europe, is that you don't have to get above the tree line to enjoy wonderful views. Mountains at similar altitudes in France, Italy, Switzerland and Austria are more likely to be covered in trees, often commercial pine, than in Spain. In these countries you can sometimes walk for days without getting 'a long view'. As in other countries Spain lost its trees (and topsoil) to agriculture and woodburning centuries ago, but because rural depopulation happened so much later trees have not yet returned to cover the mountains. There are, of course, some trees – beautiful natural ones – but not too many.

TOPOGRAPHY OF THE ROUTE

The GR1 starts near the Picos de Europa – the limestone massif that sits right in the middle of the Cantabrian Mountains, heading into Montaña Palentina and the Riaño Mountains. Although not as famous as the Picos these mountains have their own iconic peaks such as the Peña Espigüete (2451m) and Curavacas (2524m). After the Montaña Palentina comes the Burgos and Basque Mountains where the mountains are lower but just as dramatic in their own way. Depending on the 'dip' of the rock strata it's a landscape formed of escarpments, ridges, cliffs and tabletop mountains or 'mesas'. If you've walked in France you might be reminded of Jura or the Vercors, although this Spanish version is not quite as high.

So far the route has stuck limpet-like to the southern flank of the Cantabrian Mountains with occasional views across the seemingly endless central plateau to the south. Leaving the Basque Country, and the Cantabrian Mountains, this grip slips and for three days the route takes you across the flat plain of Navarre. For most people three days will be enough, but by way of compensation you pass through Los Arcos, Lagran and Olite – beautiful little towns that sit on the plain like ships on an ocean.

Escaping the plain the route climbs east again into the mountains and the Prepirinio – foothills of the Pyrenees. These foothills are formed of vast quantities of eroded rock debris washed down from the main mountain range into the Ebro valley and uplifted again in subsequent phases of mountain building. The result is a landscape of incredible variety but the cliffs (particularly those around Riglos which consist of a strange concrete-like conglomerate including water-eroded pebbles the size of potatoes) and the gorges (particularly those dissecting the Montsec range) are a special feature.

Next the GR1 crosses the north–south valleys running down from the Pyrenees and the walking is relatively arduous, with challenging daily ascents and descents. To compensate, the views of the Pyrenees are amazing, particularly if they are still covered with snow. If you're lucky with the weather, wonderful views start as soon as you leave the plain in Navarre and continue all the way to the coast.

CLIMATE AND VEGETATION

The GR1 crosses the watershed between the west-flowing Douro and the east-flowing Río Ebro not far from the walk's beginning and, after Reinosa, you stay on the northern side of the Ebro all the way to the Mediterranean.

The Cantabrian Mountains divide 'Green Spain' to north and west with its oceanic climate, and the dry plateau to the south where the climate is continental–Mediterranean with hot dry summers. Most of the GR1 follows the southern flank of the range and is therefore relatively dry although – because of the altitude – not as dry as the rest of the central Spanish plateau.

The flora is mainly Mediterranean, particularly as you approach the Pyrenean foothills where it is typical maquis or garrigue-type scrub. You walk through a beautiful but sometimes prickly mix of shrubs such as gorse, box, rosemary, thyme, lavender, rock rose and cystus. Perhaps the most characteristic tree is the evergreen oak, either the Pyrenean oak or the holm oak, often accompanied by Spanish juniper. The route also passes through beautiful natural pine and beech woods, particularly in the Basque Mountains where there are large native Scots pine forests. In the valley bottoms, if the effects of the summer drought can be avoided, there are enclaves of trees that prefer moist ground including alder, willow, ash and poplar.

AGRICULTURE AND WILDLIFE

Traditional agriculture and animal husbandry still dominate the terrain, and, while there are forests to pass through, much of the landscape is open. Expect to see flocks of sheep, sometimes mixed with goats, sometimes with a shepherd and sometimes guarded just by the huge Spanish sheep dogs (called 'mastines' in Spanish) bred since Roman times to guard against wolves. In summer in the Cantabrian Mountains you will also see herds of beautiful cattle – usually a native breed, either the dark brown Asturian valley cattle or the creamy coloured Asturian mountain cattle, and occasionally the slate grey and very ancient Tudanca breed (huge horns but gentle). Last but not least and left out in all weathers, the hardiest domestic animal of them all, the horse – usually the scruffy-looking Breton and bred (shock, horror!) for meat.

Also expect to see wild animals. The GR1 takes you through several protected conservation areas with either national or regional park status. The mountains of northern Spain are home to some of the last populations of Europe's most endangered species. The two most famous ones, unlikely to be seen, are the Cantabrian brown bear, particularly around Palencia, and the Iberian wolf, currently confined to northwest Spain but gradually extending its territory east. Other interesting and much more common mammals and include chamois, deer

Clockwise from top: Tudanca (very gentle), miniature daffodils, griffin vulture, fox at full speed, shepherd with a faithful friend

15

of various kinds, foxes, wild boar, otters, red squirrels and pine martins, and there's a chance of seeing a wild cat.

Northern Spain is also home to spectacular vultures, and the huge Griffon vulture is undoubtedly the star of the show. Most commonly found in the mountains at either end of the walk, they nest in cliffs and circle around the sky in huge numbers. If you're lucky enough to see a group of them demolish an animal carcass it's an impressive, if slightly disturbing, sight. Less common but also present are the white Egyptian vulture and the massive Lammergeier. Other raptors include the red kite and booted, golden and short-toed eagles.

Near reservoirs and on top of church towers, chimneys of houses and factories, electricity poles and almost any other tall, freestanding vertical object sit the huge nests of storks. In spring you often see multitudes of common crane migrating north in V-shaped formations, breaking their journey at the Alberca de Alboré just south of the GR1 near the beautiful Mallos de Riglos mountains. Not as big but just as impressive are the golden oriole, the hoopoe, the great spotted cookoo and the tiny Iberian chiffchaff.

HISTORY

Reconquest and reunification

Any walk through Spain could be described as a 'Sendero Histórico' but the GR1 has particular claims to the title. In a rough and ready way the route marks the boundary between

Loarre Castle (Section 5, Stage 1)

the Spain that was part of the Moorish empire and the Spain that remained Christian and visits locations that are key to understanding how the country developed. Walking the route and visiting towns and villages like Olite, Ujué, Besalú, and Loarre will give you insights into two linked processes: first the beginnings of the 'reconquest', that finally resulted in the Moors being driven out of the Spanish peninsular; and, second, Spanish unification, which eventually ended the struggle between competing elements on the Christian side. Together these developments, which started in northern Spain in the 8th century and took over 700 years to complete, finished with Spain as the 16th century world superpower.

KEY TERMS IN THE HISTORY OF 8TH TO 16TH CENTURY SPAIN

Boiling down Spanish medieval history is a very a risky task but understanding a few terms or themes will enrich your journey.

- **The Visigoths** – prior to the Muslim conquest, the Visigoths were 'in control' of Spain (defeated in France by the Franks).
- **The Muslim conquest** – in the 8th century Spain was conquered by Muslims (a mix of Arabs and recently conquered Berbers or Moors) with the Visigoths 'holding out' on the northern side of the Cantabrian Mountains in the Asturias.
- **The Marche Hispáncia** – the Muslim advance north into France was halted at the Battle of Toulouse in 721 and they were completely expelled in 759. Under Charlemagne (748–814) – a series of tiny buffer states (counties) – the 'Marche Hispáncia' (like the Welsh Marches) was established south of the Pyrenees.
- **The northern Christian kingdoms** – out of the Marche Hispáncia and the kingdom of Asturias a series of often-competing kingdoms emerge between the 8th and 10th centuries (Galicia, León, Castile, Pamplona (later Navarre), Aragón and Barcelona (later Catalonia) united for the first time, and briefly, as a single Christian entity by Sancho III Garcés the Great (992–1035).
- **Umayyad Caliphate** – from 756 to 1031 Muslim Spain was ruled as a single entity with Cordoba the capital (Abd al-Rahman I fled to Spain after the Umayyad dynasty which had ruled the whole of the massive Muslim empire had been overthrown). It reached the peak of its powers in the 9th and 10th centuries and dominated the small Christian kingdoms to the north (who typically paid taxes to the Umayyad Caliphate).

- **First Taifa period** (1009–1106) – with the fall of the Umayyad Caliphate Muslim Spain split into a series of mini-states sometimes dependent for their survival on the northern Christian kingdoms. The period ended at the start of the Almoravid dynasty who united the reduced Muslim part of Spain.
- **The reconquest** – the start of this period is traditionally dated as 722 with the Battle of Cavadonga although the real significance of that battle is that it secured the independence of the kingdom of Asturias, a significance reinforced when the bones of St James were claimed to have been found in Galicia at Santiago de Compostela.
- **The Crusades** – although usually associated with efforts to recapture Jerusalem the reconquest increasingly becomes part of the wider conflict between Islam and Christianity. With the capture of Toledo, Pope Urban II tied the conflict in Spain to his preaching for the First Crusade. From 1212 to 1295 the Christian kingdoms from the north reduced Muslim Spain (which after the fall of the Almoravid dynasty had disintegrated again into mini-states) to a rump in Granada.
- **Spanish Unification** – the marriage of Ferdinand II of Castile and Isabella I of Aragón was the basis of the unification of Spain (secured by their grandson Charles V); they captured Granada, completing the reconquest in 1492 and in 1500 enforced a policy of Muslim exile or conversion (a similar policy had been adopted towards the Jewish community in 1492)

Churches and castles

The oldest Christian churches remaining along the GR1 are in the Asturias, a region that was never fully conquered by the Moors. A distinct 'pre-Romanesque' style of architecture developed, albeit with Visigothic and Arab (Mozarabic) influences. The oldest Spanish Romanesque buildings, with their distinctive semi-circular arches, are in modern-day Catalonia where the wonderfully-named Wilfred the Hairy forced his way south and populated what had been a sort of no man's land between the Moors and Christians with monks and nuns. The famous Monastery of Santa Maria de Ripoll, built in the Romanesque style, was founded in 888.

Perhaps the best preserved Romanesque castle in the world, Loarre Castle, was built by Sancho III of Navarre ('Sancho the Great') on the site of a former Roman fortress, to defend the lands he had recently acquired from the Moors (as the Umayyad Caliphate was collapsing).

Ujué, further west along the GR1 in Navarre, whose superb defensive position was also valued by the

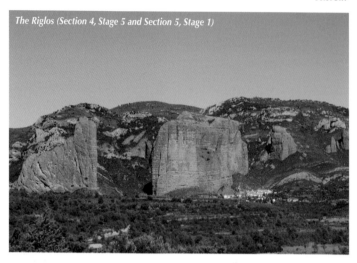

The Riglos (Section 4, Stage 5 and Section 5, Stage 1)

Romans, was subsequently developed as a hill fortress to defend Pamplona (now known as Navarre) against the advancing Moors. Its Romanesque church was built in the 11th century but then fell into decay as the Moors retreated and the site lost its value. It was later rebuilt on a lavish scale, in Gothic grandeur, as a church fortress by Charles II ('Charles the Bad') who recognised the value of the location in his power struggle with the kingdom of Castile.

Sos del Rey Católico, another stunning hilltop town, was the birthplace of Ferdinand II, King of Aragón. Built to defend land newly acquired from the Moors, it's a beautifully preserved medieval town with both Romanesque and Gothic elements. Ironically it was the marriage of Ferdinand II to Isabella I that, by ending Christian infighting, led to fortified locations like Sos del Rey Católico, Ujué, Olite and others losing their strategic significance.

It would be a mistake to assume that the larger fortified towns are the only things to excite a GR1 walker with an interest in medieval history. What is amazing, once you learn to spot the signs, is how almost every settlement has the remains of stone-built fortifications of some kind. These could be the huge square Moorish stone watch towers built on hills above villages or at the end of a valley; massive stone gates at the entrance to a village; or, more subtly, the alignment of street patterns around what would have been the defensive perimeter wall.

19

The loveliest surprise is often the sudden appearance of an old castle, a defensive tower on the side of a hill with commanding views across a valley. If you stumble upon such a place don't worry, you're probably not lost, there are just too many of them to mention them all in this guide.

While the castles and other fortifications lost much of their significance with the unification of Spain, chapels and churches continued to be used and developed. Even the tiniest village had a church and every architectural style is represented along the route – from pre-Romanesque through to neo-classical. Unfortunately nearly all the churches are locked and their treasures can be viewed only if the key holder is contacted as notice often needs to be given.

Many walkers will be happy to view the churches from the outside. If they don't know how to identify an architecture style at the beginning of the trip they should be able to by the time they have finished. The most important distinction is between the older Romanesque churches (known as 'Norman' in Britain) which have semi-circular arches and apses, and the later Gothic churches which have a pointed arch and, in bigger buildings, flying buttresses.

It is interesting to study the different styles of tympanum and sculptures that greeted the worshipper over the main door as they entered the church. The Last Judgement is a favourite subject and early Romanesque tympanums often provide graphic reminders (originally they would have been in full colour), using contemporary imagery, of the unpleasant things that would happen to the medieval sinner.

Although the principle theme of the walk is Spanish medieval history (from the beginnings of the reconquest

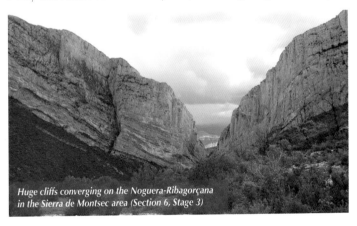

Huge cliffs converging on the Noguera-Ribagorçana in the Sierra de Montsec area (Section 6, Stage 3)

to the foundations of modern Spain) there is more on the route to interest the amateur historian. The walk finishes on the Mediterranean coast at Sant Martí d'Empúries near the site of a port founded by Greek colonists in 575BC. The remains, which are still being excavated, include the foundations of buildings and the street pattern associated with both Greek and Roman cities, making it one of the most important archaeological locations in Spain.

Industrialisation and the Spanish Civil War

The GR1 will also remind the walker of more recent aspects of Spanish history (for instance the trenches near Corconte, remnants of the tragedy of the Spanish Civil War), but what might provide the biggest surprise will be the abandoned villages in Aragón and the legacy of the rapid rural depopulation in the 1960s and 70s.

Every European country, and indeed most countries in the world, has experienced rural depopulation but in Spain it was a recent and extreme process. Compared with most western countries the impact of the industrial revolution in Spain was limited, relatively late and came to an abrupt halt with the Spanish Civil War. For two decades, the 1940s and 50s, the economy was at a standstill. Then in the sixties things changed almost overnight with industry and tourism developing rapidly and the Spanish economy experiencing a growth rate

second only to Japan. The contrast between poverty in the countryside, where many villages were still without electricity, and the opportunities in the cities suddenly became all too obvious and people, particularly young women, voted with their feet and left.

Although the effects of post 1960s rural depopulation are easy to spot all across Spain they are especially dramatic along a particular stretch of the GR1 in Aragón between Arguis and Paúles de Sarsa. The walking is beautiful with wonderful views of the Pyrenees to the north and the 2000m Guara mountain immediately to the south. The abandoned farmsteads, villages and small towns however are even more remarkable. Houses with paper still hanging from the walls and woodwork painted in colours as fresh as the day it was applied give an impression that things were abandoned overnight. It feels unnervingly like a post-apocalyptic world.

Spain continues to experience turmoil and, after the almost magical transition from dictatorship and fascism, has experienced the extremes of boom and bust. At the time of writing the recession – or the 'crisis' as the Spanish refer to it – has persisted for seven years and the impact on young people in particular is dreadful. Linked perhaps to the crisis is the other great theme of contemporary Spanish life – separatism. Confronted with an assertive presentation of different flags, graffiti and, of course, language, the GR1 traveller could easily conclude as they journey east through the Basque Country, and later Catalonia, that they are experiencing the emergence of new countries.

WHAT THE TRAILS ARE LIKE

The GR1 follows paths originally designed to link village with village that were, until recently, the main thoroughfares as the vast majority of goods were carried by people, mules and donkeys. Many of these trails are in their original state and make for perfect walking. They are gently graded and designed for getting heavy loads steadily up and over hills. Quite often the work in constructing these routes is apparent with walls (above or below), conduits to remove water and even some of the original paving still in place. The most interesting

paths are to be found in the mountains close to ancient stone villages. Here they will be walled on both sides and, just occasionally if you look closely, you can make out grooves in the carefully placed slabs of rock produced by centuries of wear from the iron rims of wagon wheels. In places a new road, capable of carrying vehicles, has been constructed to replace the original path. The old trail, with its bridges intact, is invariably more direct.

Nature is gradually reclaiming these old paths and unless they are used or maintained they will eventually disappear altogether. Centuries of wear have also turned some into gashes in the landscape – trenches – which in the winter fill with snow and mud and in the summer become overgrown with brambles. They are occasionally impassable and the

Under the Aguja Roja between Riglos and Loarre (Section 5, Stage 1)

only option is to seek an alternative route.

As with most long-distance trails there is some road walking on the GR1 but thankfully, given its length, very little. Quite often the original surface has been made accessible for farm vehicles or four-wheel drives but rarely does this generate an uncomfortable hard surface.

The GR1 is a long but easy walk. The walking is safe, does not involve any scrambling and you don't need a head for heights. It is however a walk that takes you into remote empty countryside and there are days when you are unlikely to see anyone else.

Dealing with dogs

Dogs are a feature of walking in Spain and the standard Spanish approach to keeping burglars away is to build a fence around the property and put one or more dogs inside it. They make a lot of noise and this can be unnerving. Passing through a village can trigger a dog-barking chain reaction that starts before arrival and doesn't finish until long after departure. When there isn't a fence for protection the dogs seem to change their nature and aggression ceases. Barking dogs are intimidating but a shake of a walking pole invariably puts them in their place. It may be tempting fate to say so but after thousands of kilometres of Spanish walking I am yet to be bitten by a dog.

STAYING IN SPAIN

This guide has been produced on the assumption that walkers will use the local accommodation, walk from place to place and, for their comfort,

The church tower of the submerged village of Mediano (Section 5, Stage 7)

carry the minimum amount of gear. It is possible to walk most of the GR1 and start and finish each day in accommodation directly on the route. Occasionally diversions are necessary, even a taxi journey, and where this is case the detailed notes describe what to do.

Very often the accommodation recommended is the only accommodation available. One of the joys of this kind of walking is the element of surprise involved in where you end up staying.

Broadly speaking there are two types of accommodation – provided in small hotels or by individuals.

Small hotel accommodation is described in Spain in various ways and with no great consistency. A hotel might be described as a **hostal**, **auberge** or **hotel** and the description will not give you much idea what to expect. A hostal for example, could be rooms above a bar providing fairly minimal services or it could be a lavish weekend retreat aimed at wealthy Spaniards from the city and providing a fine dining experience. Invariably the rooms are meticulously clean (the Spanish apparently use more cleaning materials per head than anyone in Europe), good value and with kind, friendly owners.

Private accommodation is usually described as a **casa rural** and again the title is not that helpful. It can mean a room in the owner's own home – similar to bed and breakfast; it can mean taking a single room in a property designed for a full property let; or it can involve a room in a property similar to a small hotel where food is provided to guests.

Where hotel-like accommodation exists this guide does not attempt to list the alternative casa rural options. Surprisingly they tend to be more expensive and are usually less fun.

There are a few places where the only accommodation available is a genuine hostel – sometimes provided by the local council – a bit like a youth hostel and where the accommodation might be in a dormitory (although chances are you will have it to yourself). Where this is the only option you will need a sheet sleeping bag and your own soap and towel.

Using the internet to find and book accommodation

There is an interesting disconnection between the information provided on websites and the reality on the ground. Many of the nicest hotels barely feature on the internet while others with sophisticated websites disappoint on arrival.

Increasingly Spanish hotels and even casa rurals are resorting to Booking.com (www.booking.com) or other intermediaries to attract customers. Some are even dropping their own websites in preference to a page on a third-party site. Small hotels are poor at responding to emails and if a lack of language skills makes using the telephone a challenge than Booking.com is incredibly helpful.

Leaving Agüero on the route to Murillo de Gállego (Section 4, Stage 5)

Accommodation listed on Booking. com is referenced in the text although it's worth checking to see whether others have moved to the site since this guide was finalised, as it's definitely a developing trend.

EATING IN SPAIN

Spanish eating arrangements may come as a surprise – every meal is eaten late. If you want an early start, unless the hotel doubles up as the local bar, an early breakfast can be difficult to organise. Common practice is to get a sandwich prepared the night before (two if they are providing you with lunch), pay, and then leave the key in the door. Lunch orders in Spain are still being taken at 3.30 or even 4pm and dinner is often at 9pm

(although the Spanish may eat even later). Interestingly dinner at a casa rural in a domestic setting is always earlier than in a hotel.

Lunch is the main meal of the day particularly on Sundays. It's often a very social event when either families or large groups of friends get together, creating a wonderful and convivial atmosphere in a restaurant. If the day's walk isn't too long a good strategy is to aim to get to your destination by mid-afternoon and enjoy a satisfying lunch.

When there is only one hotel, the food provided there is often the only food available. If you're a vegetarian you may find the options a little limited but if you're happy to eat fish or meat then you definitely won't go hungry on the GR1. Particularly good

25

are cured meats, black pudding (*morcilla*), grilled lamb and pork (often cooked on the fire in the corner of the room), beans and lentils, Spanish tortilla, and if you're early in the year wild asparagus. The food is excellent and on the route you will taste food direct from the local farmyard and food (in Catalonia in particular) that builds on Spain's reputation for culinary avant garde.

In comparison with other EU countries Spain provides excellent value for money. When walking in the mountains, accommodation with dinner and breakfast can be as little as €30 a day (and at the cheaper end of the accommodation spectrum a bottle of wine is invariably included even if you're on your own). Generally speaking the walker can easily live within a budget of €50 a day.

WHEN TO GO

Much of the route is accessible all year round but there are good and not so good times to go. Factors to consider are rainfall in the winter including snow in the Cantabrian Mountains, and the heat in the summer particularly crossing the plain in Navarre. The condition of the trail will also vary from season to season and even if there isn't a lot of snow some stretches will be so muddy that walking in winter can be uncomfortable. In addition to the weather the other factor to consider is accommodation. Much of it is available all year round

but some is not open in the winter months.

The best months for most of the walk are April, May and June and September/October. July and August are good months for walking in the Cantabrian Mountains but not on lower parts of the route. The best source of information on climate and weather patterns is the official, Spanish-language website www.aemet.es.

BREAKING THE GR1 INTO CHUNKS

This guide is designed to provide the prospective traveller with all the information needed to plan a trip along the GR1. The complete end-to-end trail is highly recommended but it does take around 53 days to complete. Most walkers will need to break their GR1 exploration down into chunks and to this end the route is described in seven sections, each with a start or endpoint that can be easily reached by train or bus. The route is described west to east. You could, of course, choose to walk it the other way but finishing at the Mediterranean adds a certain amount of drama to the trip.

Northern Spain is very accessible to the international traveller. The main options include a flight to Madrid and a train or bus journey to a section start point or a flight to a regional airport followed by train or bus. The main towns you might go through en route are often incredibly interesting in their own right (Oviedo, Bilbao, León, Burgos, Zaragoza, Pamplona) and more than justify an extended stay in Spain.

Generally speaking the train network radiates out from Madrid and information and tickets can be obtained from the excellent RENFE website (www.renfe.com). An important exception to this is the narrow gauge line that runs from León to Bilbao, a rail trip not to be missed which is also an excellent way of getting to destinations at the western end of the route.

The high-speed national coach network is also a good way of getting to section start and finish points. The largest network is run by Alsa who have a lot of regional and local buses as well. Information about the Alsa timetable is on their website (www.alsa.es) where you can also buy tickets, although this seems an unnecessary complication as you can just buy them on the day. The information is not comprehensive, however, and if a route can't be planned on their website it does not mean that it doesn't exist. Other regional operators also provide inter-city coach travel.

Tourist information in Spain is organised at various levels (national, regional, large towns/cities and important tourist destinations) and an email to the regional tourist information office usually elicits a helpful response. (See Appendix C.)

PLANNING YOUR WALK

Everyone walks at a different pace. To help plan your trip the sections of this guide are broken into stages, each as

Tozal de Guara, the highest peak in the Sierra Guara in Aragón (Sction 5, Stage 5)

close to 25km long as possible (see Appendix A for tables showing the structure of the sections and the location of facilities along the route). Also included is an estimate of how long each stage will take. This has been calculated using the famous formula developed by the Victorian walker Naismith, which allows for height gained and lost, and applying Tranter's modifications, which allow for fitness (my calculations are based on average fitness). At various points on the route you will see signposts describing how long a particular stage will take – these estimates can vary wildly and are best ignored.

Knowing that there is somewhere to sleep at the end of the day makes for a much more relaxing walk, and most people will want to book their accommodation in advance. But when there is plenty of accommodation just turning up is an option as for most of the year the hotels are rarely full. The advantage of not booking ahead is that you can be more flexible, walk longer days if the weather is really good and not have to reschedule everything if the weather is bad. Incidentally the best 'adventures' often happen when things get difficult with accommodation and you have to ask for help.

This guide includes as much information as possible on accommodation to help you plan your trip. Not all accommodation listed has been 'sampled' although where it has particular recommendations are made. Before publication contact has

Friendly accommodation at Nela (Section 2, Stage 2)

been made to check on current status but accommodation does sometimes close on a temporary or permanent basis so do check yourself if you can.

If you don't speak Spanish there is an inevitable tendency to choose accommodation which looks better organised and to book online if they have that facility or send an email if they don't. Small hotels in Spain often don't respond to email and despite the difficulty it is better to try and telephone.

WHAT TO TAKE

When you carry everything you need for the trip then weight is a key consideration. The more you carry the more strain you place on your body, particularly your knees, and the harder the walking. Unless you're carrying camping gear it should be possible to get all your gear (excluding water) in a back-pack weighing no more than 7kgs, or even less.

When packing there are a few things to consider.

- You will need proper waterproofs. Although it doesn't rain a great deal outside the winter months, when it does it can be very heavy.
- You should also take something warm, particularly if you are walking in March/April or October. Spain has the second highest average altitude of any European country (after Switzerland) and the GR1 runs through some its highest mountain ranges. It can

get very cold in the mornings and evenings and some of the accommodation will have little by way of heating.

- Included in the 7kg weight target is a sun-hat, sun-cream and sunglasses – the sun can be very strong and there isn't much shade.

This guide tells you where you can get food along the route although a good option is to ask the hotel to make you a picnic. Generally speaking they are more than happy to do this. You should carry some 'emergency rations' – you might find it's the local baker's day off, or the bar you thought was going to be open wasn't. Everyone will have his or her own emergency ration solution but a bar of chocolate hidden at the bottom of the rucksack (out of the sun and to avoid temptation) is mine.

All accommodation on the route has clean drinking water and you will be able to recharge any electronic devices you are carrying. Most places have wi-fi as well.

Think hard before taking heavy boots designed for winter walking in northern Europe. The growing consensus is that the ankle support supposedly provided by walking boots is a myth and you are definitely more likely to get blisters if your feet are hot and enclosed. The rule is that a kilogramme on your feet is equivalent to four on your back and lightweight footwear will make you more nimble and allow you to walk longer without getting tired.

FINDING YOUR WAY

As it would be for any long-distance route in Spain finding your way along the GR1 can be a challenge.

Spanish walking routes are 'defined' by the walking associations, and in Spain the regional walking and climbing associations operate to standards set at a national level. It's a voluntary activity although regional government does occasionally get involved as part of its promotion of tourism. Therefore, waymarking and the quality of the path will vary from region to region.

Waymarking on the GR1, which includes the classic French-style red-and-white paint markers, is generally good and the route is well defined in Castilla y León, the Basque Country, Aragón and Catalonia. The signs in Navarre need a lick of paint and

are non-existent on a short stretch through Cantabria.

Although the GR1 typically follows a feature (for instance a road) marked on the Institute of Geographic Information (IGN – the national mapping agency) maps, the GR1 itself, like all long-distance walking trails in Spain, is not defined on any map base. Spanish maps are therefore not that useful for a walker who wants to follow a long-distance route unless someone who knows the route has marked them up.

Using GPS technology

In addition to the route maps in this guide, it is recommended that you take a smartphone with a GPS-enabled app – an iPhone or an Android device will do the job. There are a number of GPS apps available

Waymarks in Castilla y León (Section 1)

but perhaps the essential requirement is the ability to buy and download Spanish maps through the application. The range of apps that provide this facility is growing all the time.

A good example, and the app used in the research for this guide, is Viewranger. The Viewranger website includes a map store which has a growing portfolio of maps from around the world including Spain. You can download the IGN 1:25,000 maps for the whole route at a fraction of the cost (and weight!) of paper maps. Viewranger's default mapping – OpenCycleMap – is available at no charge. Included in the Viewranger route library is the GR1 route produced as part of the research for this guide, which can be downloaded and then displayed against the mapbase on a smartphone. The route is in a format that can be used on any GPS system and can also be displayed in Google Earth.

GPX tracks for the route can also be downloaded for free from the Cicerone website once you've bought this guidebook (www.cicerone.co.uk/member).

While many walkers have a smartphone it is surprising how many don't use GPS. If you haven't used the facility don't leave it to the last minute before your trip to Spain to find out how it works. Smartphone GPS doesn't use data roaming so you don't need to have the potentially expensive international data roaming facility turned on. The battery on

the smartphone should be adequate for a day's walking particularly if you remember to turn off any facilities that you're not using. (Many people have their phone permanently searching for a wifi connection and that facility is a particularly heavy battery user.) If you are nervous about battery life than take a charged battery and reload on the way or, if you are walking with someone else with a smartphone, have a duplicate version of the GPS as backup.

Most of the route is waymarked and generally speaking you wouldn't need to use a paper map very often and similarly the GPS will be needed only on an infrequent basis. When a waymark has been missed however the GPS will show you where you are relative to the route, making getting back on track very straightforward. With Viewranger the GPS will provide directions on an ongoing basis but this consumes the battery and given the waymarks it's a facility you don't need.

If you are already an expert GPS user and have your own device then the Spanish maps on the IGN website are free to download for non-commercial use.

After completing the research for this Guide I can state with some confidence that the GPS route provided for the GR1 is the most up-to-date and accurate route available. I would not however claim 100 per cent accuracy. Route descriptions in this guide point out where the route has been hard to find and where there is the greatest degree of uncertainty. Even after several trips and the advice of local experts, mistakes can be made. The route also changes, either because locals want to bring walkers to their village or occasionally because landowners want to see them off. However, even if the route recommended doesn't follow the latest on-the-ground version of the GR1, it will get you to the Mediterranean.

USING THIS GUIDE

The 1250km of the GR1 are described here in seven sections, each one broken into stages roughly 25km in length. Sections begin with an introduction and summary information, and each stage begins with an information box – giving basic data such as start point, distance, ascent, descent, maximum altitude, walking time and grade – and a short introduction to give you a feel for the walking ahead of you that day. There follows a step-by-step route description, with extra information about any facilities available along the way and other points of historical, geological and natural interest. Each stage is accompanied by a clear, contoured route map at scale of 1:100,000 and features common to both the map and the description are highlighted in bold within the description to help you link the two.

The route maps in this guide are derived from publicly-available data, databases and crowd-sourced data. As such they have not been through

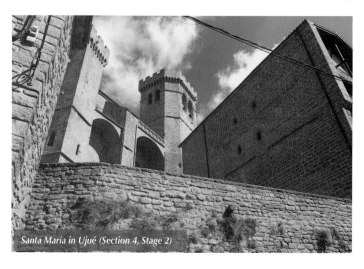

Santa Maria in Ujué (Section 4, Stage 2)

Olite (the end of Section 3 and start of Section 4)

the detailed checking procedures that would generally be applied to a published map from an official mapping agency, although naturally we have reviewed them closely in the light of local knowledge in the preparation of this guide. If you spot any errors or possible improvements please let us know by email to updates@cicerone.co.uk.

Stage grading

The pleasure of 'through-walking' – walking every step of the way from A to B – is not universally shared. Not everyone has the time or inclination and will want to choose which bits of the route to do with the time they have available. To help you make that choice, a grading system has been used. The first element measures the quality of the waymarking and the second the wow factor – a necessarily subjective judgment.

Quality of waymarking goes from 0 to 5:
- 0 = non-existent
- 1 = occasional signs only
- 2 = poor, rarely helpful
- 3 = helpful but use with care
- 4 = good with only occasional gaps
- 5 = excellent, proceed with confidence.

Wow factor goes from 1 to 5:
- 1 = poor, only a through-walker, completer-finisher would do it
- 2 = OK, but could be avoided if time is short
- 3 = good, fine walking including memorable highlights
- 4 = excellent, not to be missed but with occasional lesser stretches
- 5 = excellent, worthy of an international trip in its own right.

1 PUERTO DE TARNA TO REINOSA

Peña Espigüete from the southeast (from Stage 1.4)

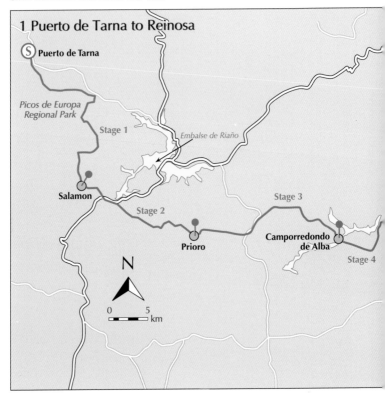

1 Puerto de Tarna to Reinosa

S Puerto de Tarna

Picos de Europa
Regional Park

Stage 1

Embalse de Riaño

Salamon

Stage 2

Stage 3

Prioro

Camporredondo
de Alba

Stage 4

N

0   5
km

In terms of landscape the first stage of the walk is one of the best. The route crosses the southern flank of the Cantabrian Mountains, skirts the Picos de Europa and passes through two protected areas: the Regional Park of the Picos de Europa and the Natural Park of Fuentes Carrionas and Fuente Cobre-Montaña Palentina. It's a stunning limestone landscape and includes a number of summits over 2500m high. The star of the show is Peña Espigüete, passed on Stage 3. Although it's not the biggest mountain (at 2150m) it is the most admired and the one that attracts the climbers. It has an almost perfect shape, stands slightly apart from the rest of the Cantabrian Mountains, and dominates the scenery for most of the section.

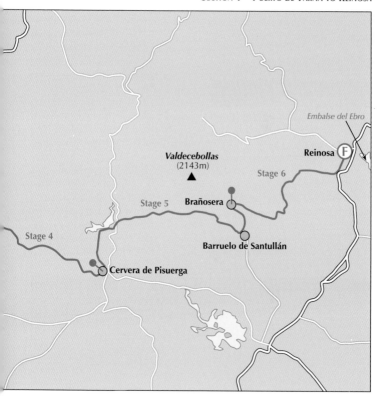

Although the scenery is dramatic the trail is easy and the waymarking excellent. The GR1 is supported by the Castilla y León regional government and there are signs and information boards from the Puerto de Tarna through to Brañosera where the route crosses into Cantabria. It is, however, remote: services are few and far between and accommodation, particularly at the western end, is sparse. For this section booking in advance is essential if only to check that the accommodation is open.

From a historical perspective and compared with the others, Section 1 is perhaps less interesting but the landscape and natural habitat provide a ready compensation. Although you're unlikely to see one of the resident Cantabrian brown bears you will see the Cantabrian Chamois, possibly otters and wild cats, and definitely vultures, particularly the huge Griffon vulture.

ACCESS AND ACCOMMODATION

The best way to get to the start of the route – Puerto de Tarna – is by bus from Oviedo. Oviedo is a lovely city particularly famous for its pre-Romanesque buildings the best of which – Santa María del Naranco and San Miguel de Lillo – are located just out of town. These both featured in the Woody Allen film *Vicky Cristina Barcelona* and Allen's praise of the place means he is now a local hero and honoured with a city centre statue. The easiest way to get to Oviedo for international travellers is via Asturias airport or, a bit further away, Santander. Alternatively you can fly to Madrid and catch a train.

Reinosa is much less interesting than Oviedo and, for most travellers, would not justify an extended stay. It is, however, particularly well connected: to Santander (a bus every hour); to Bilbao and León one bus each way a day; and Madrid (two trains a day). If you are continuing on the GR1 from here, you could easily press on to Corconte (the start of the second section) by bus when you finish walking Stage 6.

SECTION 1: KEY INFORMATION	
Distance	158.5km
Total ascent	4950m
Total descent	5650m
Alternative schedule	Consider staying in the hostel in Trilollo and exploring walks around the Curavacas – see Stage 2.

STAGE 1
Puerto de Tarna to Salamon

Start	Hospedería de Salamon, Puerto de Tarna (1509m)
Distance	28km
Ascent/Descent	560m/1040m
Grade	4/4
Walking time	8hr 50min
Maximum altitude	1585m
Access	From Oviedo, by bus up to Bezanes (in the Alto Nalon and Natural Park of Redes) and a taxi up to the pass itself. All being well you should be able to start walking by 11.30am. From Bezanes, ask Rafael, the taxi driver who owns the casa rural there (see www.clubrural.com), to take you up in the morning.

An excellent first day, great scenery, long with a pass to climb over in the middle but not a tough walk. There is a bar in Manaña but it doesn't provide food. If you want a shorter first day than there is accommodation at Manaña.

Puerto de Tarna is a pass that sits on the regional boundary between Asturias and Castilla y León. On the right-hand side of the road at the pass is an information board about the Regional Park of the Picos de Europa (easily confused with the National Park of the Picos de Europa which is located immediately to the northeast and contains the main part of the Picos de Europa range). The highest mountain in the Picos, Torre Cerredo (2648m), is about 6km from the pass as the crow flies.

Although there is a restaurant it is not always open and not to be relied on.

Follow a path for 600 metres heading directly south from the pass on the right-hand side of the valley, parallel to a road on the left-hand side, and descend for 600

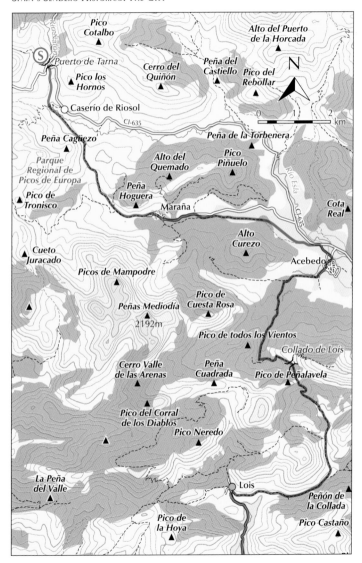

metres across open moorland to the unoccupied hamlet of **Caserío de Riosol**. Pass the church and head down to a fountain and picnic area just below the hamlet and join a dirt road heading southeast. The signs at this point direct you along the PR-19. ▸

PR indicates a short walking trail, 'Sendero de Pequeño Recorrido' in Spanish.

The route follows the south side of a valley with open pastures to the left and the **Picos de Mampodre** to the right.

Stay on the dirt road, cross a low pass and head down into **Maraña** nestling under the cliffs of the **Peña Hoguera**. The views south of Peñas Mediodía (2192m) from within the village are excellent.

Maraña has a bar, a very small shop and cabin-style accommodation at the Cabañas Patagonicas (see **www.booking.com**).

Head east out of Maraña along the main road for about 600 metres. Leave the road just beyond footpath signs heading north, cross an old bridge and continue east along the edge of pastures to the little village of **Acebedo**.

Parque Regional de Picos Europa

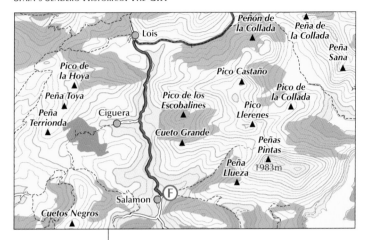

The route enters Acebedo avoiding the main road and crosses a bridge over a small river in the village centre. Head southwest out of the village up an ever-steepening dirt road and follow it west for about a kilometre, towards the **Peñas Mediodía**. Turn south, staying on the same dirt road, and head up a valley into increasingly dramatic mountains. After 5km the dirt road splits. Turn left here and climb in an easterly direction. The landscape becomes open and moor-like with amazing views back into the **Picos de Mampodre**. Just before the top of the pass, leave the dirt road, which heads north up to the top of the ridge, and turn south to the pass, the **Collado de Lois**.

Cross the pass and follow a well-defined path down, initially through trees, and then across open pasture, to a stream joining a route that comes down from a refuge to the east. Follow a path running along a tight valley, initially along the side of a stream, and head south, then west, all the way to the hamlet of **Lois** in the centre of which stands a large baroque-style church (called the Mountain Cathedral, Catedral de la Montaña, for its size compared with the small village).

From Lois follow a road east and then south, through a narrow gorge with a river running along the bottom, through **Ciguera**, all the way to **Salamon**.

Salamon is another tiny village with accommodation in a casa rural, the Hospedería de Salamon (987 710 806, www.hospederiadesalamon.es)

STAGE 2
Salamon to Prioro

Start	Hospedería de Salamon, Salamon (1114m)
Distance	19.5km
Ascent/Descent	1020m/970m
Grade	3/4
Walking time	7hr 20min
Maximum altitude	1583m

Although not long, Stage 2 crosses three passes and a tackles a significant amount of climb. Apart from Las Salas there is nowhere to stop on the way so start early and aim to get to the Prioro in time for a late lunch.

Turn right from the Hospedería de Salamon and walk down the road to a bridge. Cross the bridge and turn right, head northeast through Salamon and climb along a concrete road to the edge of the village and take a right fork up the side of the valley. The trail zigs-zags its way steeply up through trees before levelling out on the final approach to the pass, the **Collado del Pando**.

Cross the pass and follow a path that switches from the left-hand side of valley to the right before descending down along a beautiful old track. It passes a 'chozo', a traditional thatched shepherd's refuge, and heads down through evergreen oaks, Pyrenean or holm, to the village of **Las Salas**. ▶

Watch out for deer in the trees.

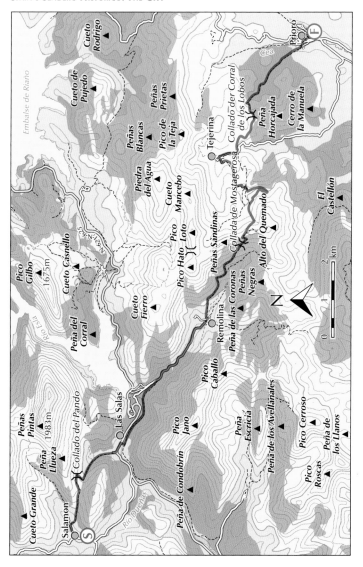

Las Salas is a small village located on the first significant road on the route. There is accommodation
and food at the hostal/bar, Hostal las Pintas (987 71
08 33) and the rural tourism centre, the Centro de
Turismo Rural Vegalion (see **www.booking.com**).
There are also signs there for St James's Way.

*Crossing the
Collado del Pando*

Follow the road past the hostal, turn right and cross
the bridge over the **Río Esla**. Head east alongside the
river. After a kilometre, on the other side of the river, the
great wall of the dam that holds back the waters of the
Riaño reservoir should be visible.
Leave the river and follow a path alongside a stream
to a bridge and onto a road. Follow the road for 2km to
the village of **Remolina**.

Remolina has no shops but it does have a particularly ugly modern church grafted onto the foundations of a much older one.

In the centre of the village, at the fountain, turn left
off the road joining an ancient path that leaves the village

45

and heads up through trees along the north side of the valley. It's a beautiful climb with great views through gaps in the trees to the limestone cliffs on other side of the valley. 800 metres from Remolina, and after 200m of ascent, the route reaches a gate where the path splits: take the left fork. ◄ By the time you have reached the pass, the **Collada de Mostagerosa**, you will have climbed nearly 500m.

There is a particularly good viewing point just before the gate.

From the top of the pass, to the east, you can just see Tejerina the village in the bottom of the next valley. Although it doesn't look far the route to it is indirect. After the pass leave the dirt road and follow a path through broom and scrub. Initially it's easy to follow but as it turns directly down the valley side, alongside a stream, it becomes overgrown, and the waymarks are difficult to find. The waymarks re-emerge about 100 metres below the point at which the route follows the stream but on the other side.

The GR1 then contours around the valley heading south and away from Tejerina along a dirt road before switching back on itself along an ancient tree-lined path towards the village. After 600 metres cross a dirt road and continue north through a pasture. The waymarks are again difficult to follow. After 200 metres, and on the other side of the pasture, the route runs alongside an old wall, a path and irrigation canal heading east and down towards **Tejerina**. Approaching the village the path merges with the irrigation canal and the route will almost certainly be wet and muddy.

Tejerina is a small village with no services. Watch out for the work of a local sculptor who has had some fun with the drinking fountains.

Arriving at the church, follow the road south out of the village for about 200 metres and turn left off the road onto a path. The path climbs gradually around an open hillside, heading south, before turning and crossing the pass, the **Collado der Corral de los Lobos** (site of an ancient wolf trap). On the other side of the pass the route joins a dirt road that it follows all the way down to **Prioro**.

Prioro is a village with a limited range of services including a cafeteria/bar 'El Pando', a restaurant 'Las Conjas' and a bread shop. There are three casa rurals that provide rooms on a nightly basis – the Molino de Prioro (987 71 55 12), the El Cueto Apartmentos (987 533 477) and the Casa Rural El Serrano (659 97 56 45) – the last two are both available through Booking.com.

STAGE 3

Prioro to Camporredondo de Alba

Start	Calle la Iglesia, Prioro (1075m)
Distance	24.5km
Ascent/Descent	960m/810m
Grade	4/4
Walking time	8hr 40min
Maximum altitude	1606m

A wonderful walk with huge open stretches dominated by views of the Peña Espigüete. There is nowhere to eat on the way so either take lunch or plan for a late one at Camporredondo de Alba.

The main street through Prioro is called Ctra Pedrosa. At the junction with Calle la Iglesia head east (opposite the Calle la Iglesia) and follow the road as it swings north on the west side of a valley to a dirt road and GR1 waymarks.

After 400 metres the dirt road divides. Take the right-hand fork over a bridge and head east. After a further 50 metres, cross another small bridge, ignoring a road to the left, turn right and leave the main dirt road (that continues on along the valley). Cross a bridge over the river and climb up the farm road on the southern side of the valley. After nearly 3km and 200m of climb the route reaches the top of the pass.

Crossing the pass the waymarks are a little confusing but the GR1 runs east down the valley and parallel to a

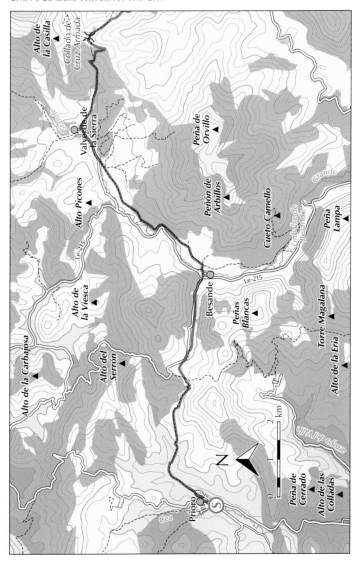

road visible from the top. From the pass it dives through a gap in some gorse bushes and then turns down the valley before eventually meeting the road that takes you into **Besande**.

> **Besande** has a fine 13th-century Romanesque church and an example of an *hórreo*, an ancient wooden grain store built on a stone plinth. There are also signs to a restaurant but it wasn't open the last time I visited.

Leave the village on its eastern side, cross a bridge over the Río Grande, head northeast along the valley, parallel with the main road on its the western side. After about 3km the trail veers east into a wider valley dominated at the end by Peña Espigüete. The next village, 2km further on, **Valverde de la Sierra**, appears to sit underneath the mountain.

> **Valverde de la Sierra** has a pretty Romanesque church but no services. It sits on the boundary

Looking east towards Peña Espigüete from Collado de Cruz Armada

49

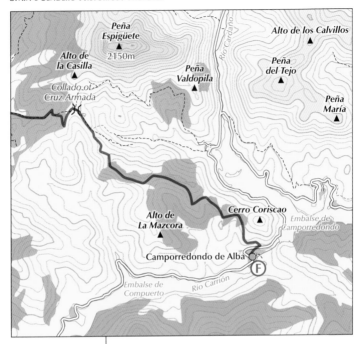

between Parque Regional de Picos de Europa and the Parque Natural de Fuentas Carrionas y Fuente Cobre.

Take the road east out of the village (it turns into a dirt road and swings east) along a flat-bottomed valley. After about a kilometre, the road disappears and the route follows a trail through scrub up the side of the valley to the ridge. Head north along the ridge to the pass, the **Collado de Cruz Armada**, enjoying amazing views of **Peña Espigüete**.

The GR1 then stays high, heading southeast for another 5km on an easy-to-follow dirt trail before making on a gentle descent down to **Camporredondo de Alba**. The views on this last part of the walk are excellent.

Camporredondo de Alba is a pretty village located immediately beneath a dam to the reservoir named after the village. It has two restaurant/hotels: the Meson el Abuelo (979 86 60 34); and the Hostal Restaurant Tia Goya (979 86 60 32). Both serve local food and the Tia Goya is open all year round.

STAGE 4

*Camporredondo de Alba to
Cervera de Pisuerga*

Start	Meson el Abuelo, Camporrendondo de Alba (1250m)
Distance	30km
Ascent/Descent	680m/900m
Grade	4/4
Walking time	9hrs 20min
Maximum altitude	1433m

Apart from a 5km stretch of road walking, this is another excellent stage with great views, particularly early on. There are several options for lunch stops (and wild water swimming), particularly towards the end.

From the hotel(s) head east to the trees in the village centre and down the bridge over the **Río Carrión**. ▶ After 200 metres take the left fork before a bridge over a stream and head along a dirt road up the valley past a series of buildings containing beehives. Follow the dirt road as it turns north and head downhill over a cattle grid to a junction with other paths, cross it and carry on into ever-improving scenery.

Watch out for otters in the river.

> **Peña Espigüete** (2150m) is now to the west of the trail and **Curavacas** (2525m) to the north. In the foreground is the **Embalse de Camporredondo** (reservoir).

51

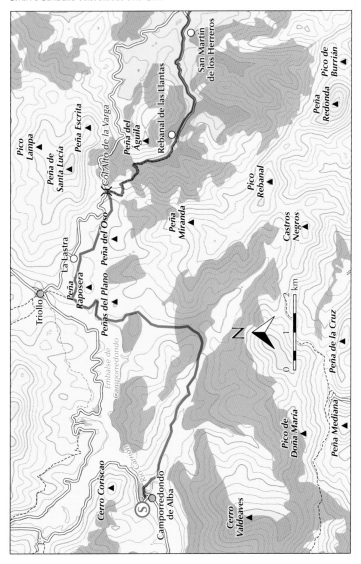

The trail continues north above the banks of the reservoir, crosses a bridge and then splits with a variant heading onto **Triollo**.

Triollo has one hotel, the Hostal Rural La Montaña (979 866 171) 3km to the north of the village and Hostel Curavacas (979 866 223) which is a available through Booking.com.

The main GR1 turns right at the junction with the variant and heads east across open moorland to **La Lastra**, a hamlet with no services. Turn right in the centre of the village and follow a small road heading south and take the first left along an old tree-lined trail going east along a shallow but pretty valley which, depending on the time of year, will be full of cattle. The route passes underneath power lines and becomes a little steeper as it climbs up to a road, a picnic spot and some information boards at the **Col Alto de la Varga**.

The Col is at the foot of **Peña de Santa Lucía** a steep limestone mountain with views of the Río Carrión valley and the Montaña Palentina range to the west. To the south is the Peña Redonda, the bear reserve and Tosande, a remote yew forest.

The route then turns abruptly south and for about 400 metres follows a ridge before turning east again. It then descends along a steep path into a densely wooded gorge. ▶

The cliffs above the gorge provide an ideal place for nesting vultures and there is every chance they will be out patrolling the skies.

From **Rebanal de las Llantas**, join the road for the next 5km to the other side of the village of **San Martín de los Herreros**. Unfortunately neither village has any services to compensate for the hard surface walk.

Turn right off the road 300 metres after San Martín de los Herreros, cross an old bridge and follow the edge of a water meadow along what must have been the old road to **Ventanilla**. ▶

Instead of crossing the main bridge, head through a farmyard immediately to the south of the road and climb

On the north side of Ventanilla is a bar but if you can wait an hour the options are much better at the next village, Ruesga.

Looking north to Curavacas

up onto the path just next to one of the farm buildings. Follow the path alongside the **Embalse de Ruesga** (where,

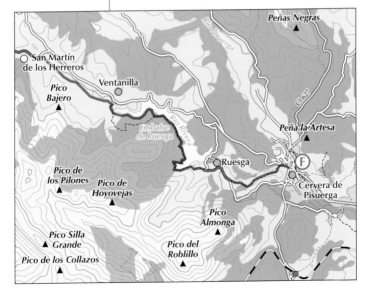

if it's hot and the weekend, the locals will be having a swim) all the way to **Ruesga**.

> **Ruesga** is a pretty village sitting underneath a dam and has a bar and two restaurants. The Hotel Rural Casa María (979 870741) is a particularly good place to eat, serves local specialties and has rooms. One of Spain's famous parador hotels, the Cervera de Pisuerga, sits high above the village with famously great views.

Cervera de Pisuerga is only 2km further on, has lots of accommodation and, because of the distance to Brañosera (the next stopover), is perhaps the better place to aim for. To get there head east for 300 metres along the road, turn left onto a dirt track and follow it to the town.

CERVERA DE PISUERGA POPULATION 2461

Cervera de Pisuerga is a scruffy town but if you're travelling west to east is the place to find the first of the GR1's historical gems. The most important one is the church of Santa María del Castillo passed on the way into the town. The building as a whole is late Gothic (16th century) and at one time served as a medieval fortress. It's impressive from the outside but the real gems are inside and include an altarpiece from the Spanish-Flemish School by Felipe de Bigarmy (part of the funeral chapel of Santa Ana) and the main altarpiece constructed in a Renaissance style. You need to book in advance to visit (606 145 0045). To the south of the town, just before the village of Vado, are the remains of the San Vicente Hermitage, an 8th-century 'building' carved out of a rock and surrounded by graves (happily empty), also carved out of rock.

The town has the full range of services with several small hotels the best of which is probably the Hostal Peñalabra (979 970 037; www.hostalpenalabra.com) – very traditional, comfortable and with excellent food. The Hotel Roble (979 874 429; www.hotelelroble.com) – a modern hotel – serves early breakfast which is helpful if you want a fast getaway in the morning. Both hotels can be booked at www.booking.com.

STAGE 5

Cervera de Pisuerga to Brañosera

Start	Calle San Roque, Cervera de Pisuerga (1054m)
Distance	33km; shortcut: 27km
Ascent/Descent	1440m/1240m; shortcut: 1130/930m
Grade	4/4
Walking time	11hr; shortcut: 9hr 30min
Maximum altitude	1603m

Another great walk with wonderful views, particularly towards the end. The shortcut is recommended but if the route is still too long then stay at Estalaya. If you're going the whole way organise a sandwich for lunch.

Head north through the town along the main street (Calle San Roque). Continue north as the main road swings east, stay on left-hand side of the **Río Pisuerga**, passing through a new municipal park, along a path between playing fields and the river, past an old water mill and into open countryside. Stay on the left-hand side of the river until it crosses an old bridge into the village of **Arbejal**.

> **Arbejal** is a small pretty stone village with a youth hostel (979 87 01 74).

To the west the Curavacas should be visible.

Leave the village on its northern side, passing the church (which blends at its end into an old house). Cross the main road about 200 metres to the north of the village and join an old dirt road on a gentle ascent. ◀

Take care. The waymarking is also a little obscure as you approach the village but it can be found if you look carefully.

At the top of the pass, leave the dirt road and head along a path through a beautiful forest of Pyrenean oak. After descending almost to edge of the **Embalse de la Requejada**, passing the remains of what looks like an old lookout tower, head east through trees to the village of **Vañes**. For the first 400 metres the route crosses the hillside, descending steeply to the reservoir. ◀

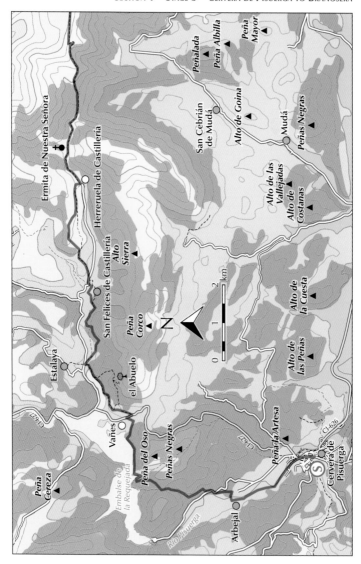

Instead of going into Vañes turn right at the main road and left onto a dirt road after 100 metres. The route then takes you above the village with views to a church, bedecked with storks' nests, and the multi-arched road bridge over the end of the reservoir. It then turns east into the Castillería valley.

> At the top of a small incline a footpath turns up through the trees to the ancient El Roblón de Estalaya oak, possibly the oldest oak in the Cantabrian Mountains and affectionately known as **el Abuelo** (Grandpa). It rejoins the GR1 after a kilometre.
>
> 800 metres after the sign up to el Abuelo there is **GR1 variant** to Estalaya (10mins) and the Océano Verde rural tourism centre and a hotel with a restaurant (979 184 354; **www.oceanoverde.org**).

The main GR1 continues on along the Castillería valley and, through the trees, to **San Felices de Castillería**.

The waymarking is hard to follow especially on the final approach to the village. There are also barbed wire 'gates' that need a bit of patience particularly if you are walking alone. As you get closer to the village the signs disappear altogether but beware as the obvious direct route is wet and boggy and is avoided only if you approach the village from the southeast.

> **San Felices de Castillería** has a pretty church (San Pedro Advinculan) but no services.

The route leaves the village to the east and climbs gently along a dirt road from where, looking back, there are views of Peña Espigüete.

Towards the top of the hill above San Felices de Castillería, the route leaves the dirt road and follows a path through a forest of low evergreen oak so dense that it feels like a tunnel. The tunnel traverses its way around the top of the hill before joining another dirt road that it follows down into the village of **Herreruela de Castillería**.

The population of **Herreruela de Castillería**, which feels like a large farmyard, is only 19 people, but if you're lucky you might be able to persuade someone to open the cantina. The calendars on the wall are interesting but perhaps not to everyone's taste. The church of St Miguel is 16th-century Gothic but the most impressive historic building is the solid half-timbered farmhouse that sits at the top of the hill.

Peña Espigüete and Curavacas

The route carries on east out of the village along a dirt road, past the Romanesque **Ermita de Nuestra Señora del Monte**, and then crosses to the south side of the valley and starts a long climb (nearly 500m) to the top of the pass.

Shortcut direct to Brañosera

At the top of pass there are some electricity pylons and at this point you can choose to take a fast route down to Brañosera saving 5km and over an hour of walking.

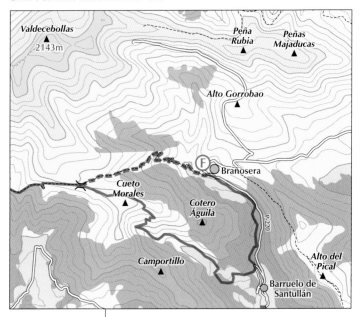

The views are already good by the time you get to the pass but actually get better as you climb a little along the official route.

> If the weather is good the views of **Peña Espigüete** and the **Curavacas** will be amazing. To the south-west the point at which the Cantabrian Mountains end and the apparently endless plain of Castile begin should be clearly visible. If you have the time, than a walk up **Valdecebollas** (2143m), to the north-west of the pass, will provide views of the whole Picos de Europa range.

The official GR1 route carries on from the pass along the ridge, heading east for about 1.5km before descending down a mountain road into a valley.

The valley was an important part of the **Palencia coalfield** but lost its market when Spanish trains abandoned steam in the sixties. On the way down to the old mining town Barruelo de Santullán, the GR1 passes a coalmining museum although this was closed the last time I was there. When the mines stopped working the population of the town shrank from over 8000 to less than 1500.

Barruelo de Santullán has a hostel, the Casa de la Gota (979 60 61 84; **www.casadelagota.com**) and a restaurant El Carmen (979 18 13 45).

The route doesn't actually go into **Barruelo** but heads north up a valley through trees to **Brañosera**. If you have walked all the way from Cervera de Pisuerga you will be wondering at this point why you didn't take the shortcut when you had the chance.

BRAÑOSERA POPULATION 284

Brañosera is a small town with 284 inhabitants and is particularly important in terms of the promotion of the GR1. Its mayor runs a website (http://gr1.branosera.com) and every year the town hosts a conference to discuss the route's development.

For its size it's particularly well endowed with hotel/restaurants and accommodation and the chef at the Restaurante Hostal Cholo (**www.hostalcholo.com**) has a reputation for excellent food. If you can't get into the Cholo, which is sometimes busy, then try the Hostal Restaurante San Roque (979 607181). My favourite place in Brañosera is the Meson Cueva del Coble – a wonderful quirky restaurant run by the charming and well-travelled Jesus Garcia Delgado. You can't miss it – it flies the Canadian flag.

STAGE 6
Brañosera to Reinosa

Start	Town centre, Brañosera (1205m)
Distance	24km
Ascent/Descent	530m/890m
Grade	0/3
Walking time	7hr 40min
Maximum altitude	1219m

An easy walk, predominantly downhill and there should be plenty of time to get to Reinosa for lunch and to catch the bus if the aim is continue on and stay at Corconte.

After a wonderful passage through the high Cantabrian Mountains the GR1 fizzles out as it crosses the regional boundary from Castilla y León into Cantabria. The route was maintained for a while but the regional walking association no longer supports it and the waymarks are literally fading away. Apart from a visit to the impressive Argüeso Castle the original route has little to recommend it and it involves a lot of road walking. An alternative route is described here which takes a more direct route to Reinosa.

After following the main road (marked with GR1 signs) west through the village, turn north along a dirt path to the cemetery. The route then follows a dirt road which contours round the valley heading east, above Brañosera and the main road. After a kilometre join the main road and go east along it for about 200 metres where the route splits into two variants. Ignore the one which goes along the road to **Salcedillo**, and instead take the dirt road across open moorland to the southeast. Continue along the dirt road for 5km and follow it as it climbs over the moor and drops into a wide valley (the Valle de Valdeolea in the Cantabria region). After 5km the route turns north.

After 600 metres the route crosses a bridge. The official GR1 probably continues north at this point but

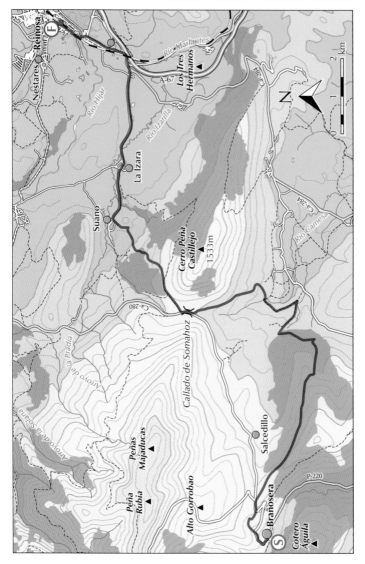

63

our route turns east just past the bridge and crosses the regional boundary into Cantabria. Follow a farm trail for about 300 metres, with a stream at the bottom of the valley on the right-hand side, turn left and climb gently up a valley heading north. After 600 metres cross the valley on a bridge and climb the side of a hill (heading east) to a new dirt road which takes you north to the main road and the pass at **Callado de Somahoz**.

From the pass head down the main road for about 300 metres, turn off the road and follow local footpath signs along a route described on the map as the Camino de Brañosera. Head down the valley in a northeasterly direction to the village of **Suano**, join a small road and go through the village of **La Izara** and then on to Matamorosa, immediately to the south of Reinosa.

REINOSA POPULATION 9804

Travelling west to east Reinosa is the first town on the route with good train and bus access making it an excellent place to start or finish a stage of the walk. It's a substantial town and has a selection of hotels and other services. Developed in the 18th century after the construction of a bridge over the Río Ebro, Reinosa is located just to the south of the official source of the river and to the west of a huge reservoir bearing the river's name. Although the town has no buildings or monuments of national significance it has an attractive town centre and, for the first time on the trail, features houses with large elaborate covered balconies – a common element in Cantabrian architecture.

The town has a number of hotels including the Hotel Vejo (942 751 700; **www. hotelvejo.es** and **www.booking.com**) and the Hotel San Roque (942 754 788; **www.hotelsanroque.eu**).

2 CORCONTE TO BERANTEVILLA

Looking west to Tuesta

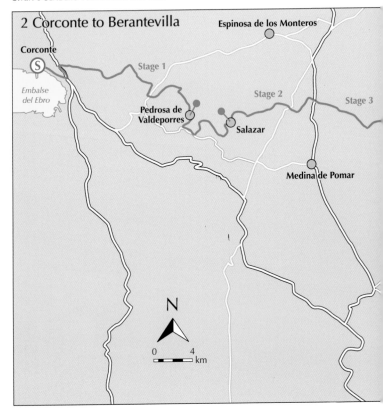

This section of the GR1 involves a gentle walk through the limestone landscape of the eastern Cantabrian Mountains. It's similar to the Ardeche in France and includes some of the same distinct features including the deep gorges, natural bridges and underground caves. The landscape makes for easy walking and there is plenty to see.

The route passes through a series of small villages and crosses the northern part of Burgos, a province within Castile and León (although it briefly enters and leaves the Basque Country and the Vaderojo Natural Park). It visits: a series of beautiful, often very intimate, little churches; the town where written Spanish is believed to have originated; one of the oldest

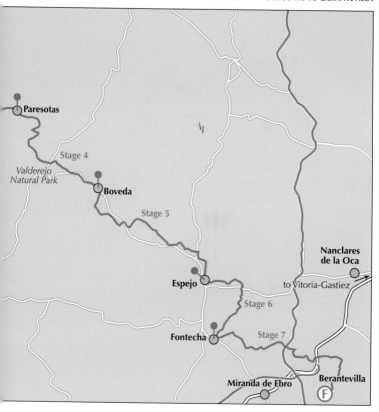

and most important salt works in the whole of Spain, if not Western Europe; and a temporary resting point for the Holy Grail.

Starting in Cantabria the route then re-enters Castilla y León (the province of Burgos) before entering the Basque Country (the province of Alava). The boundary between the Castilla y León and the Basque Country is particularly complicated and the route crosses it several times.

ACCESS AND ACCOMMODATION

The 175km of walking described here has been broken down into seven stages. Transport connections are via Reinosa at the western end and

67

Miranda de Ebro at the eastern end. Miranda de Ebro is easy to get to by train or coach from both Bilbao or Madrid.

To avoid a long road walk out of Reinosa, the recommended start point is Corconte (or, if you need to save a day, Pedrosa de Valdeporres). The daily Bilbao bus leaves Reinosa mid-afternoon and there is a stop just past the village. If the first two sections are being walked together there is plenty of time to walk from Brañosera to Reinosa, catch the bus and start from Corconte the next day.

The penultimate stage to Fontecha is only 16km long. There is no accommodation on the last stage and if you want to complete the route you will have to leave it, to stay at Miranda de Ebro or Rivabellosa, and return to continue the walk. Alternatively you could finish the section at Fontecha or walk another 20km to Armiñón and catch a bus to Miranda de Ebro or Vitoria.

Although the connections to Miranda de Ebro are excellent there isn't much to see in the town itself. Vitoria, one stop on the main line to the north, is much more attractive, with an interesting medieval town centre. It was the location of Wellington's final major victory over the French in the Peninsular War, a victory undermined slightly by the drunken celebrations of the British Army. The town is well worth a visit and if you're travelling from east to west it is possible to get a bus to Fontecha and start your walk there.

SECTION 2: KEY INFORMATION	
Distance	175km
Total ascent	4410m
Total descent	4569m
Alternative schedule	Consider staying 2 days at Salazar and exploring the Canales and visiting the Complejo de Ojo Guareña – see Stage 2.

STAGE 1

Corconte to Pedrosa de Valdeporres

Start	Conchita restaurant, Corconte (841m)
Distance	23km
Ascent/Descent	550m/700m
Grade	3/2
Walking time	7hr 30min
Maximum altitude	1015m
Note	Corconte is still in Cantabria and lack of GR1 maintenance shows.

Stage 1 is a pleasant easy walk spoilt slightly by a stretch along a concrete road through a wind farm. There are places to eat at Pedrosa de Valdeporres or just down the road at Santaelices.

CORCONTE POPULATION 48

Corconte sits on the banks of the Ebro reservoir and has some particularly fine stone houses despite being a small village. The area became fashionable in the late 19th century when the local waters were believed to have medicinal properties and some of the buildings date back to that period.

Excellent value accommodation is available at the Restaurant Conchita (942 77 83 51; www.restauranteconchita.com) – located near the road. The alternative is the Balneario de Corconte, a huge and much more expensive spa hotel just down the road (947 15 42 81; www.balneariodecorconte.es and www.booking.com).

Official GR1 route – not recommended
Head east past a fortified entrance to a farmstead and through a gate. Faint GR waymarkings are visible on a wall nearby. The route then heads up the hill alongside a fir plantation to the right and a fence to a field on the left. There are power cables running up the hill. The route is extremely overgrown and almost impassable.

A welcome waymark

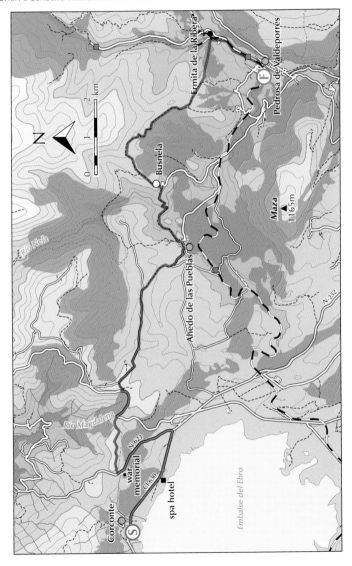

The alternative and recommended option (marked on the route map here) is to walk east along the main road from the Conchita restaurant, past the **spa hotel**, turn up the hill at the first left and join the track just to the north of the sign announcing the Province of Burgos. At this point the route is not waymarked and to escape the dense shrub you have to walk through the pasture beyond the fence on top of the hill.

> Once in the pasture, watch out for **trenches** running east to west. These were dug by republicans in the Spanish Civil War and mark a line designed to defend the road to Reinosa. The 'pyramid' opposite was built after the war to accommodate 300 Italians who died trying to capture the hill.

Follow the brow of the hill eastwards, descend into a valley and join a dirt track heading north down to a road. Pass through a gate onto the road and follow it east. Just as the road turns north, GR1 signs on the right-hand side point east and into a huge wind farm.

The route is now well waymarked and follows a new concrete road eastwards.

> Despite the wind farm the views ahead are excellent particularly the **Canales de Dulla**, a large tabletop mountain which sits on plateau which itself has been cut into by a gorge. It looks like a giant layer cake.

After 4km leave the concrete road and follow a path down to a dirt road into the village of **Ahedo de las Pueblas**. Although small, it's another village like Corconte with grand stone houses. Near the pretty church dedicated to San Nicolás Obispo is a bar, the 'El Corral de Los Gallos', which may be open if you're lucky.

Leave the village along a path to the right of the church and follow a dirt trail into a valley full of low scrub-like vegetation. Descend down the valley, across a river and climb up the other side to the tiny settlement

Breton ponies protest against windfarms

Looking south you should be able to see a castle, the Torre Castillo en Cida.

of **Busnela**. Leave the hamlet along the dirt road heading northeast and then south for 3km. ◄

After 3km the dirt road splits, take the left-hand fork and head directly east. 300 metres further on leave the path, which turns south, and continue east through trees and down the valley to a little chapel, the **Ermita de la Ribera**.

Just beyond the chapel is a narrow gauge railway with a service once a day from León to Bilbao. Also running on the line is the **El Expreso de la Robla** (although it no longer goes to la Robla), sister to the more famous (and more expensive) El Transcantábrico – the line that runs along the north coast of Spain. El Expreso de la Robla travels along the longest narrow gauge railway line in Europe, a line built to carry coal from León to the steel mills in Bilbao replacing more expensive imported Welsh coal. It takes a stunning route through the Cantabrian Mountains and the Basque Country and attracts train buffs from all over the world.

Head south, following the railway line, through St Martín de Porres to the larger village of **Pedrosa de Valdeporres**.

Pedrosa de Valdeporres has accommodation at the La Casa Engaña, (947 13 80 73; **www.laengana.com**) a language school located in the centre of the village.

STAGE 2

Pedrosa de Valdeporres to Salazar

Start	Bus stop, village centre, Pedrosa (680m)
Distance	22.5km
Ascent/Descent	700m/800m
Grade	4/4
Walking time	7hr 10min
Maximum altitude	1022m

Stage 2 is a lovely, easy walk through beautiful limestone country full of stunning villages. The highlight is Puentedey, famous for its natural stone arch. Organise your lunch before setting off as there is nowhere to eat on the way.

From the bus stop, cross the railway line and the bridge over the **Río Engaña**, turn onto a trail through a grass field and, after 200 metres, cross the abandoned Santander–Mediterráneo railway to a road. Cross the road and start a steep ascent to a pass in the cliff face, **El Portillo**.

On the top amongst the evergreen oaks the way-marks are hard to follow but after 200 metres heading in a southeasterly direction the route emerges into open ground and onto a dirt road and turns north. ▶

The views of the cliffs of the Canales de Dulla are excellent.

Follow the dirt road to the lovely village of **Villamartín de Sotoscuera** nestled underneath the limestone cliffs.

73

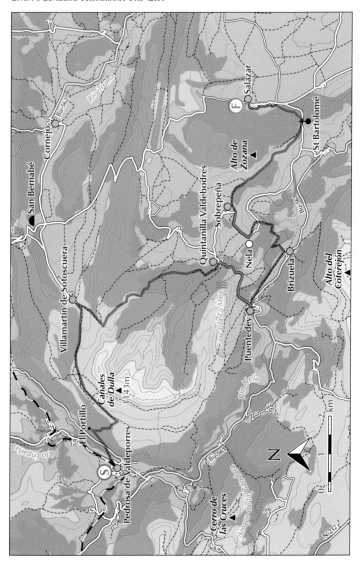

Under the Canales de Dulla

Not on the route but just a kilometre or so further west are the church caves of **San Bernabé**, known as Complejo de Ojo Guareña, the eyes of Guareña. These 13th-century 'buildings' are a national monument and well worth a visit.

Just before the village of Villamartín de Sotoscuera the route heads abruptly southwest and climbs up a dirt road to a pass. On reaching the pass, leave the dirt road, descend into the gorge and follow it to the village of **Quintanilla Valdebodres**. Depending on the time of year the stream at the bottom of the gorge could be full of water, and the route runs first on one side then the other.

Quintanilla Valdebodres is a stunning village with a number of beautifully preserved buildings including the Romanesque church, the Iglesia de San Miguel Arcángel, and a watermill.

Follow the road south out of the village to **Puentedey**. ▶

In the cliffs on the right-hand side you should be able to see a waterfall, Cascada La Mea.

75

Puentedey

Puentedey is a gem. It sits on top of a huge natural bridge that spans the Río Nela and is much larger than the more famous Pont D'Ardeche in France. The settlement features an 11th-century Romanesque church, the Church of San Pelayo, and a medieval palace, the Palacio de Los Porres. There is a tunnel through the limestone arch providing direct access from the village to the river below. There are no services in Puentedey.

Crossing the man-made bridge over the **Río Nela** follow an abandoned railway line east to the village of **Brizuela** (whose Romanesque church is dedicated to St Christopher). Head north through the village to the river, turn west, cross a footbridge, and continue east along the riverbank, through a gorge, to **Nela**.

Although only a tiny hamlet **Nela** is home to the lovely Manzanela – a rural tourist centre run by an Anglo-Dutch couple who provide good food and accommodation (692 472 163; **www.manzanela. com**).

The views from here are wonderful.

Passing through Nela, head west across a field and up onto a quiet road. ◄ Continue east past a church, across the junction and join a dirt road (the road continues north

76

to **Sobrepeña**). Follow the dirt road (which turns into a path), head south into a lovely valley and cross it after about 500 metres. Climb the valley on its eastern side to a pass and a road.

> Perfectly located on the pass is a **chapel** dedicated to St Bartolomé, a beautiful Romanesque building with mozarabic influences.

Cross the pass and take a path heading northeast. **Salazar** is about a kilometre away.

> Salazar is a lovely little village full of fortified Romanesque houses and palaces and with three churches, some with Moorish elements. The La Ondina casa rural provides bed and breakfast at the edge of the village (947 13 14 78; www.laondina.com). Medina de Pomar is 11km away, has lots of accommodation and is well worth the visit. Hotel Restaurant La Alhama (947 190 846; www.hralhama.es) can be reserved through Booking.com. For a taxi ring Alex (654 563 341).

STAGE 3

Salazar to Paresotas

Start	Village centre, Salazar (650m)
Distance	31.5km
Ascent/Descent	640m/610m
Grade	4/3
Walking time	9hr 50min
Maximum altitude	750m

The Salazar to Paresotas stage is long but easy. It visits a series of small villages, although only Torme has a bar, so remember to ask for a packed lunch from your overnight stop.

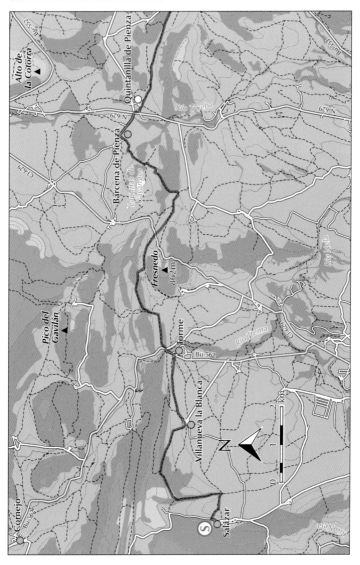

Join the main road on the eastern side of the village and follow it north to the village's edge. Turn right off the main road and head east down a tree-lined farm trail. After 500 metres, turn north onto a narrow road and continue for nearly a kilometre climbing gently onto a limestone escarpment with views south across a flat arable plain. Leave the road and head east through low evergreen oak before dropping down to the little village of **Villanueva la Blanca**.

After Villanueva la Blanca continue east and climb once again towards the escarpment, arriving at the village of **Torme** after a kilometre or so. The route leaves Torme along the main road, past the Romanesque church dedicated to St Martin, over a bridge, and turns off the road heading east through a pretty little valley.

Climb out of the valley and continue east through open countryside crossing a road after 2km.

Just over a kilometre later the trail splits. Take the left fork, turn northeast and descend, eventually, into a wide flat valley with lots of dairy cattle and on to the village of **Bárcena de Pienza**. Before reaching Bárcena you can see in the distance the **Lagunas de Gayangos**, natural lakes in the plain that provide a unique wetland habitat for waterfowl.

Lagunas de Gayangos

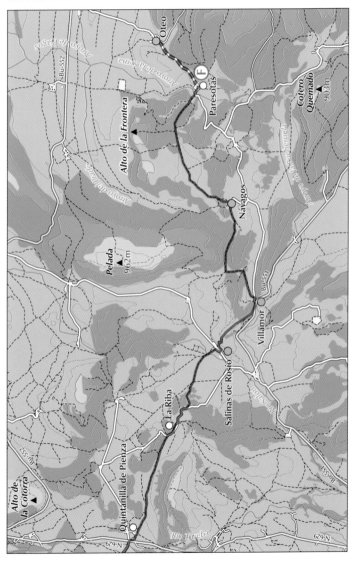

Head east along a road, across a fine 16th-century bridge over the **Río Trueba** and into **Quintanilla de Pienza** (whose large Gothic church is dedicated to St James). ▶

Leave Quintanilla de Pienza and continue east taking a very narrow, deep and potentially muddy cattle trail. Depending on the time of year it might be necessary to leave the trail and walk in the field alongside. Continue east along the dirt road for 3km where the route joins a small road and heads down into **La Riba**, another tiny village.

Continuing east out of the village the route leaves the road, heads down through trees and across an open plain to **Salinas de Rosío**, another village whose fine old stone houses suggest a more illustrious past.

Salinas de Rosío is situated on the western side of a rocky gorse-laden limestone ridge. Cross the village, pass an ancient stone fountain and follow a path southeast along the flank of the ridge to a road and head east into **Villamor**.

Leave the road in the village and follow an agricultural road northeast. After 1.5km take a right fork and continue for another 1.5km into the tiny village of **Návagos** dominated by a large medieval defensive tower.

Head northeast, then east, out of the village crossing an increasingly scrubby landscape and descend down into the village of **Paresotas**.

The Paresotas accommodation is actually at Oteo situated 1.5km along the road to the northeast. The owner of the little hotel – Los Perrichicos (947 195 073) can be persuaded to pick you up if you haven't the energy for an end-of-day road walk.

The village has no services but does sit alongside a main road and a bus route to Bilbao.

STAGE 4
Paresotas to Bóveda

Start	Village centre, Paresotas (700m)
Distance	23.5km
Ascent/Descent	630m/630m
Grade	3/4
Walking time	7hr 30min
Maximum altitude	901m

The highlight of an easy walk is the visit to the beautiful little church of San Pantaleón de Losa. Again there is nowhere on the route for a lunch-stop so take a picnic.

You may be able to persuade the owner of the hotel in Oteo to give you a lift back to Paresotas to rejoin the route.

◀ Follow the main road south through the village. On the edge of the village the GR1 leaves the main road and follows a dirt track heading south down a hill, over a bridge across a small stream and up to a cemetery. The cemetery is about 200 metres from the village.

Just beyond the cemetery turn east entering pine woodland after another 400 metres. Follow a meandering trail for 6km (southeast and southwest) before finally emerging at the small village of **Pérex de Losa**.

Leave Pérex de Losa on the main road heading south and stay on it for 400 metres; turn east along a dirt road, cross an open field and climb a gentle ridge into trees. After following the dirt road in a semi-circle north, then south, leave it and head south across an open field and another dirt road. Walk south through trees for about 400 metres, along the eastern side of a gentle valley and emerge onto a path above a gorge. Turn east and descend down to the bottom of the gorge, passing under large power lines along the northern bank of the river to an old medieval bridge and cross it.

The gorge is the result of sharp meander in the course of the Río Jerea. The meander has left an outcrop of limestone – the **Peña Colorada o del Santo** – on top of which sits, in dramatic isolation, a church dedicated to San Pantaleón de Losa.

Consecrated in 1207 **San Pantaleón de Losa** is regarded as one of the best examples of Romanesque art in Spain. The arch surrounding the main door is particularly interesting. The statue on the left-hand side features the mythical figure Atlantean while the figurative decoration of the capitals include warnings to the sinful (a snake devouring a fallen man) and references to the story of Jonah and the whale.

The building is also linked to the complex legend of the Holy Grail. One version has the Grail in Northern Spain during the time of the Crusades and San Pantaleón de Losa is one its three possible resting places.

San Pantaleón de Losa

83

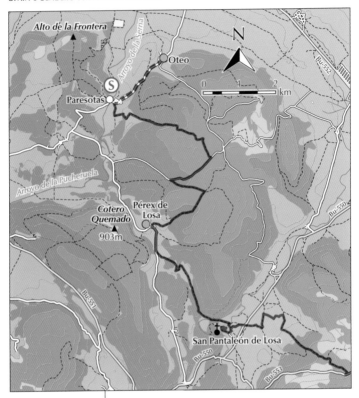

The views looking back to the Peña Colorada o del Santo are even more dramatic from this perspective.

Returning from the Peña Colorada o del Santo, head back down through the tiny village of Barrio de Arriba but instead of crossing the bridge over the **Río Jerea** take the right-hand fork, head northeast and then east to the main road. ◄

Cross the main road and continue east along a dirt road for about 400 metres until it meets another dirt road running north–south. At this point the waymarks are a little confusing and a short connecting part of the trail has probably been lost. Follow the waymarks and head north for 300 metres, then turn east, cut across the field (about

300m) and join up with the dirt trail on the other side before heading south.

After 100 metres or so, depending on when you cross the field, the trail leaves cultivated land and enters trees. Ignore the left-hand fork, head southwest, then southeast and carry on in this direction, through trees and climbing, for 2km to the main road.

The route is crossing a limestone ridge and the pass, the **Puerto de la Horca** (the Pass of Gallows) is 200 metres further along the main road (where the GR1 enters the Basque Country (Euskadi)). The route then descends steeply down the other side of the ridge, possibly following an older version of the road, heading first across open karst countryside and then down a steep trail running parallel with the main road. After a kilometre, and a drop of 200 metres, the route once again hits the main road.

The quickest way into **Bóveda** from this point is to follow the main road. The waymarks however leave the road, follow a trail through the trees directly south and along a route that, if followed, will bypass the town.

Bóveda has two places to stay: the Neitha Puelles, a small hotel with restaurant (945 356 011; **www. neitheapuelles.es**); and the Casa Rural Herranetxe (945 353 182 and 670 234 534). There are also buses from the town all the way to Vitoria.

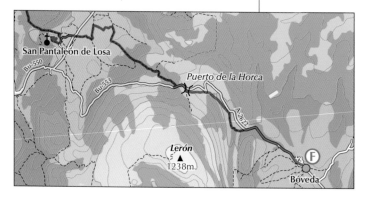

STAGE 5
Bóveda to Espejo

Start	Village centre, Bóveda (680m)
Distance	28km
Ascent/Descent	820m/1010m
Grade	4/4
Walking time	9hr 10min
Maximum altitude	804m

The scenery is best during the first half of this stage with the cliffs of the Peña Gobia a dramatic feature. For once you don't need to pack a sandwich and instead can stop for lunch at the restaurant in the beautiful village of Valpuesta.

Cross the bridge over the river and follow the farm trail southwest towards the cliffs of the Sierra Bóveda and **Peña Gobia**. After crossing arable land climb gently through trees almost to the cliffs before turning southeast down to the little village of **Tobillas** and the main north-south road.

> **Tobillas** is a beautiful stone village with a lovely Romanesque church dedicated to St Roman.

Continue southeast out of the village for about 800 metres before turning northeast across the valley and the main road. A short waymarked detour from the route takes you up to some 4th-century hermit's caves (described as 'artificial' because they were carved out of the rock) complete with burial chambers.

Back on the main trail, continue southeast before turning almost 180 degrees around the end of small ridge, and heading northeast up a valley. After 600 metres head down to a road and turn right. After 15m on the road turn left onto a trail and follow it up to the village of **Pinedo**.

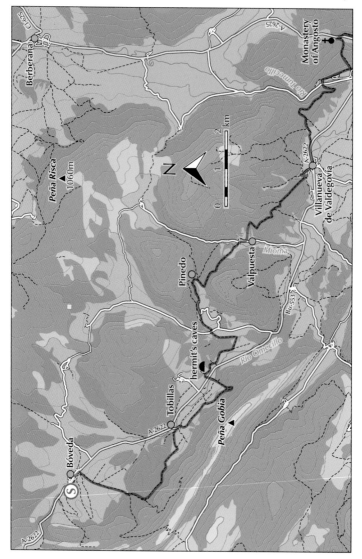

4th-century hermit's caves

Continue south past Pinedo, enjoying the views back to the Peña Gobia, climb a pass (about 200 metres higher than the road below Pinedo) and then drop down into a wooded valley. Nestling in the valley, about 1.5km to the southeast, is the beautiful village of **Valpuesta**.

VALPUESTA POPULATION <20

Valpuesta gives its name to two documents (the Cartularies of Valpuesta) which are thought to include the first words written in Spanish. The village is home to a bishopric dating back to 804AD and contains several important buildings. These include the Collegiate Church of St Mary (a national monument which hosts some significant Renaissance works of art), a large defensive tower and a beautiful half-timbered building called the Canons.

There is also a smart restaurant that, according to the website, has accommodation (947 353 620; **www.loscanonigos.com**).

Don't miss the great views back to the town as you climb.

Head out of Valpuesta on the main road and, before the edge of the town, take a sharp left turn and join a path and follow it up the side of the valley into trees. ◄

The route continues southeast for another 3km and drops down into **Villanueva de Valdegovía** where the town hall confirms emphatically that this is local administrative centre but there isn't much to detain a visitor.

The route carries on east along the main road and turns left onto a trail about 400 metres from the town centre. Climb up onto a ridge and down into a valley to the **Monastery of Angosto** where a shepherd, Hernando Martin, saw an image of Virgin Mary in 1089 and created, in an instant, a must-see medieval pilgrim destination. It's a pretty spot although the Gothic church has been heavily restored.

Cross the river near the monastery and head south along the eastern side of the valley past a campsite, turning east after 400 metres. Cross another woody ridge, descend into a valley, cross a main road, and head south and then east through uninspiring scrubby countryside. Turning south, head into a shallow arable valley. 3km from the Monastery of Angosto the route arrives at the village of **Villamaderne**.

To the northwest of Villamaderne is Villanañe, home to the **Torre de los Varona**. Made up of a manor house and a tower, this fortified home of the Varona family perched on a hilltop, is a spectacular

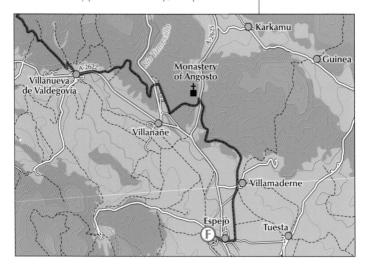

example of medieval military architecture and parts of it may date back to the 7th century.

From Villamaderne continue south for 1.5km to **Espejo**.

Espejo is a scruffy little town straddling a busy road. It does, however, have a number of fine buildings including more fortified houses. There are food shops, a couple of restaurants, bars and a cash machine. Accommodation may be available in a small hotel although this was closed on the last visit and the modern youth hostel (945 351 150) was a more than adequate alternative. If a hotel is preferred than there is small one in Tuesta, the next village on the route, about a kilometre away (945 351 496; **www.hotelruralamona.com**).

STAGE 6
Espejo to Fontecha

Start	Village centre, Espejo (490m)
Distance	16km
Ascent/Descent	360m/260m
Grade	4/4
Walking time	4hr 10min
Maximum altitude	696m

This is a short, easy stage, necessarily so because of limited accommodation in the next stage. The highlight is the visit to Salinas de Añana where there is a restaurant if a lunch option is needed. It is possible to extend the day by walking on to Villabezana and leaving the route to stay at Rivabellosa but the recommended option if you are going straight on to Section 3 is to stay at Miranda de Ebro for two nights and use taxis and public transport from Fontecha and Berantevilla (see box) to cover every step of the GR1 in between.

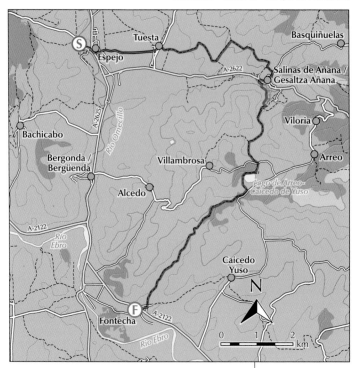

The route leaves Espejo the same way it entered but instead of turning north to Villamaderne continues east for 1.5km towards a low ridge and the village of **Tuesta**.

> The village church at Tuesta, dedicated to the **Nuestra Señora de la Asunción** is stunning and cited as one of the best examples of the transition from Romanesque to Gothic styles. If you can't get inside, the doorway alone is worth the visit. The decoration portrays a series of angels and human beings, wild beasts and monsters, birds and vegetables and delivers messages designed to keep the worshipper on the straight and narrow.

From Tuesta, and after crossing the main north–south road, the route meanders in an easterly direction across an undulating landscape along a well-defined agricultural trail. After around 5km it enters **Salinas de Añana** from the north.

SALINAS DE AÑANA POPULATION 165

Salt pans at Salinas de Añana

One of the oldest towns in the area, Salinas de Añana owes its strategic importance to the extraction of salt and the vast array of saltpans – wooden terraces – step their way along the tight valley immediately south of the town (Valle Salado – 'Salt Valley'). It's a very interesting place, slightly surreal, and there are plans to restore it and achieve Unesco World Heritage Site status.

The Añana Palace is a very good restaurant, but it may be a little early for lunch (945 567 968; **www.ananaturismo.com**).

Head down through the town, past the church, and south along the valley to the western side of the saltpans. Climb out of the valley and follow a small road south for about 1.5km to leave it and continue south as the road turns west. After 400 metres descend down through holm oaks to the **Lago de Arreo-Caicedo de Yuso**, an important stopover for migratory birds.

From the lake continue south heading gently down along a pretty valley for about 5km to the village of **Fontecha**.

Fontecha's strategic end-of-valley location, defending the route to the Salinas de Añana, left it bedecked with not one but two fine medieval defensive towers, the Constable Tower and the Tower of Orgaz. Unfortunately it has little else to recommend it, although the bar will be open if you're lucky.

STAYING AT MIRANDA DE EBRO

If the goal is to walk every step of the GR1 and the intention is to go immediately onto Section 3 then the best option is to stay at Miranda de Ebro for two nights. After arriving at Fontecha get a taxi to Miranda de Ebro (or hitch a lift, a very feasible option) and return next day to complete Stage 7 to Berantevilla. There is an early morning bus from the train station in Miranda de Ebro to Fontecha so a taxi is only needed one way. As there is no accommodation in Berantevilla return to the hotel in Miranda de Ebro at the end of Stage 7 for the second of two night's accommodation.

Mirando de Ebro has several modern hotels all located near the train station. These include the Tudanca Miranda (947 311 843; www.hoteltudanca. com and Booking.com) and Hotel Achuri (947 34 72 72; www.hotelachuri. com and Booking.com). For a more atmospheric option consider the Hotel Hospederia el Convento (947 332 652; www.hotelconventomiranda.com and Booking.com). Fontecha is 11km from Mirando de Ebro and if a taxi is preferred to hitch-hiking contact Taxi Miranda (619 568 887; www.taxis miranda.com).

STAGE 7
Fontecha to Berantevilla

Start	Village square, Fontecha (490m)
Distance	30.5km
Ascent/Descent	710m/750m
Grade	3/2
Walking time	9hr 30min
Maximum altitude	706m

Stage 7 involves crossing a major north-south transport corridor with railway lines and motorways. It's not as bad as it sounds although falling for the temptation of a more direct route to Miranda de Ebro would be understandable. Despite the number of villages visited there is nowhere for lunch.

Head east along the northern side of the main road, take the first left and continue east across the low valley to

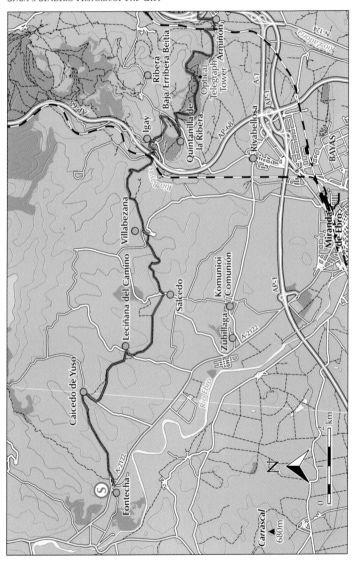

the church (retracing the route at the end of the previous stage). Follow an old road just below the church and to the north of the eastern tower. Climb gently along the northern side of a valley and, after 600 metres, turn left at the fork. 2km from Fontecha and just after passing a ruined church, join a slightly larger road and continue into the village of **Caicedo de Yuso**.

From the village centre take the main road south. After about 100 metres, on the village edge, turn left and follow a trail east and out into open countryside. The route, overgrown at times, follows the edge of a field southeast. 600 metres after leaving the village join an access road to a solar panel installation and head down to a country road. Follow this southeast for another 400 metres into the tiny village of **Leciñana del Camino**.

Take the main road south out of the village and turn left after about 50 metres, heading southeast and following an old overgrown trail. Turn east after 400 metres and join an agricultural road. After another 400 metres, and before the village of **Salcedo**, there is a GR1 sign pointing north. Ignore it (it sends you on a purposeless detour) and continue into the village.

Following the waymarks again, leave Salcedo on its northeastern side and continue east along a dirt trail for 700 metres before turning right off the dirt road (which continues north). Head east, south and then east again along the side of a field to the village of **Villabezana**.

Accommodation is available at Rivabellosa at the Hotel Julia (945 35 50 42; **www.hoteljulia.es** and **www. booking.com**). On the northern outskirts of Miranda de Ebro, Rivabellosa is reached by a 5km detour along the road that leaves Villabezana on its south side.

The GR1 leaves Villabezana on its eastern side and, after crossing a road, takes the left-hand fork on a dirt track and continues east. Follow this track for 2km, across and then south into down a valley. At the bottom of the valley the route takes a bridge over a railway line, turns left and after 100 metres passes underneath a motorway.

San Estaban at Quintanilla de la Ribera

It then turns south before crossing a bridge over the **Río Bayas** and turns immediately north, through trees, along a narrow path up out of the valley to the pretty little village of **Igay**.

Leave Igay on the road heading south, leave the road after 90 metres and follow a path down to the village of **Quintanilla de la Ribera** with its lovely Renaissance church dedicated to San Esteban. After dropping down through the village join a dirt trail heading northeast, cross a valley, turn south and then east.

The route passes a tower, part of a 19th-century **optical telegraph network** and one of an original line of 52 that ran across Castile.

Leave the tower and join a dirt trail which heads northeast and then starts a steep descent east out of the trees before turning south. In open countryside it then heads east and down to **Armiñón** arriving after passing underneath a main railway line and crossing a wonderful medieval bridge over the **Río Ibaia**.

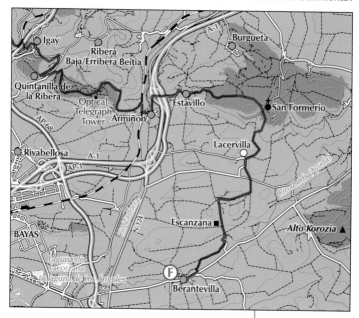

Armiñón, another lovely village with some grand stone buildings, is spoilt by the proximity of the motorway. It does however have a restaurant (although not open when I was last there) and bus routes to Vitoria and Miranda de Ebro.

Ignoring some old waymarks (which predate the motorway) head north and underneath the motorway via a couple of large roundabouts and climb up to the village of **Estavillo**. There also signs here for the St James Way, on its way south from Vitoria.

Exit Estavillo on its eastern side at first on a road, and take a path through trees up towards a **chapel** dedicated to San Formerio and a TV mast. The route leaves the path before it reaches the summit and heads steeply down a ridge and into open countryside but it is worth making the short detour to the chapel to savour the views.

After 300 metres join a dirt road and follow it south to the tiny village of **Lacervilla**. Initially leaving along a road, join a path immediately south of the village and stay on it for 200 metres before reaching a junction with a dirt track. Continue south along the dirt track for 200 metres, turn west at a junction with another track and follow it for 600 metres before turning south at a junction with yet another track. After 1km the route arrives at the farmstead of **Escanzana** and joins a road that heads down to a bridge. Before crossing the bridge turn east along the northern bank of a river, past a watermill and on into the village of **Berantevilla**.

Berantevilla has a bar and a restaurant but unfortunately no accommodation.

The only place to find accommodation is back in **Miranda de Ebro** for which you need to take either a taxi or a bus. The quickest way to get a bus involves a 5km walk. Take the road west out of the village until it reaches a busy road heading north–south. Walk south along this road for about 500 metres and then turn west past a service station and over the motorway. After crossing the bridge there is a bus stop for a shuttle service into the city centre and the railway station.

3 BERANTEVILLA
TO OLITE

The door to the Santa Maria church

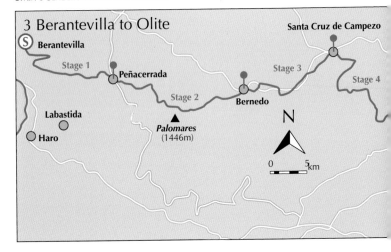

3 Berantevilla to Olite

The route from Berantevilla to Olite falls into two halves: the first runs through wild remote countryside along a limestone ridge on the northern side of the Ebro valley and the second crosses the wide-open vistas of the plain of northern Navarre. If you've walked all the way from the Cantabrian Mountains the plain will come as a shock – it's the first significant stretch of flat walking since the start of the GR1. It doesn't last long however and within a few kilometres of Olite the route is back in the mountains.

Beware that the waymarking deteriorates when you leave the Basque Country and enter Navarre. The waymarking in Navarre has been bleached by hot summer sun and literally needs a new coat of paint.

The route visits interesting historic settlements. In the mountainous western end the towns/villages are small and tightly defended and contrast with the larger more self-confident towns on the plain. Olite in particular is one of the highlights of the whole route – beautiful and carefully preserved – and comparable with Carcassonne in France.

ACCESS AND ACCOMMODATION

The walking is easy and the section as a whole can be broken down into manageable stages, although at the western end accommodation choices are limited.

Olite is very accessible and works well as an end point for the section. It's particularly easy to get to by train or coach from Bilbao via Pamplona, or from Zaragoza or Madrid. It also has

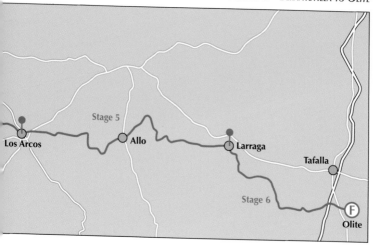

a wonderful parador – an excellent representative of Spain's most famous hotel chain located, as these hotels often are, in an ancient and lovingly restored building. If you have been walking for days and feel you deserve a treat, this is the place to get it.

Many will find the two-day walk from Los Arcos to Olite a bit dull.

Larraga, the suggested stopover, is pleasant enough but the countryside either side of it is the least interesting of the whole of the GR1. If pushed for time with no great need to walk every step to the Mediterranean, than a bus to Olite from Los Arcos via Pamplona is a good option.

SECTION 3: KEY INFORMATION	
Distance	161km
Total ascent	4060m
Total descent	4130m
Alternative schedule	The Santuario de Nuestra Señora de Codés, visited in Stage 4, has interesting accommodation with lots of local hikes.

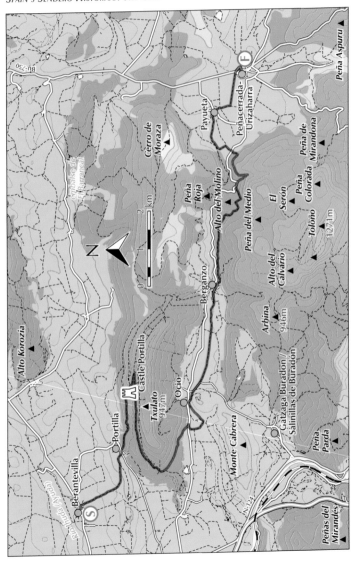

STAGE 1

Berantevilla to Peñacerrada

Start	Town centre (just north of church), Berantevilla (440m)
Distance	22km
Ascent/Descent	930m/660m
Grade	3/4
Walking time	7hr 40min
Maximum altitude	846m

There is no accommodation in Berantevilla so getting to the starting point will involve either a bus to the edge of Miranda de Ebro and an unpleasant 5km walk, or a taxi. Once you get to Berantevilla it's a pleasant walk but there is nowhere to stop for lunch.

Head east on the main street and just before the car park turn right and head south out of the village along the De Fracales Kalea. Continue south for about 600 metres, along an agricultural road across flat fields, before climbing and turning east. After another 400 metres, and after passing a cemetery, the route arrives at the village of **Portilla**.

> Portilla is a small village with no services – overlooked by that the ruins of the almost inaccessible **Castle Portilla** which recent research suggests was built on a site inhabited in the Iron Age, possibly earlier. The castle was of such importance in medieval times that it is represented as a central motif in the shield of Alava and legend claims that beneath it is buried a golden bull.

Cross the road that cuts through the village and follow the dirt road heading east, climbing past some interesting limestone rock formations. Continue for another 2.5km. After a 300m ascent (from Berantevilla) the route

Lanos Castle at Ocio

reaches a pass, crosses into a wooded valley, and starts to descend in a westerly direction. On southern side of the ridge views of the **castle ruins** are excellent.

Follow the valley down for 3km as it turns from west to south. After 3km leave the agricultural road and follow a path east across the side of the valley, descending to a road after 1.4km.

To the east, sitting on a hill, is a perfectly located castle.

◄ Cross the road and follow a path through fields at the bottom of the valley, heading first south then east on a roundabout route to the village of **Ocio**.

Ocio is a small village overlooked by **Lanos Castle**, impregnable on three of its four sides – a weakness spotted by Sancho IV of Castile who sacked it from that fourth side in 1284.

From Ocio, head east along a flat dirt road through fields along the bottom of the valley. The little village of **Berganzo** is reached after 3km. There are no services but a pretty church dedicated to San Miguel provides partial compensation.

Continue east from Berganzo and climb gradually up through an increasingly narrow wooded valley. After 2kms the route turns south up a side valley, climbs a small ridge on its eastern side and then drops down again to the road in the main valley. From the top are good views of Sierra de Cantabria. After crossing a second side valley to the south and completing another climb, head north leaving the trees, and cross the road and join an agricultural road to the village of **Payueta**. ▶

Payueta is a small village which has a particularly good example of a public laundry.

Leave Payueta on its southeastern side. **Peñacerrada**, 2km away to the southeast, should be clearly visible.

PEÑACERRADA POPULATION 269

Peñacerrada (also marked as Urizaharra on some maps) was fought over a number of times and it still has its medieval defensive walls. Particularly impressive is the south gate, two huge semi-circular towers topped with a matacán. Other significant buildings include: the church, which was one of the richest in the province, originally Romanesque with a particularly fine altarpiece; the palace of the Dukes of Hfar built in the late 17th century; and the 18th-century water mill on the edge of town which is still in full working order.

The ground floor of the mill is a bakery and accommodation (no dinner) is also provided on the upper floors (945 36 71 14; **www.nekatur.net/errota**). The village has a bar/restaurant – the Restaurant San Prudencio (+ 34 945 36 70 43) – but no other services. There is an ethnographic museum full of artefacts illustrating how the locals used to live. If the mill is fully booked then accommodation is also available in a casa rural in the nearby village of Barola (945 367 075; **www.elrincondebaroja.com**).

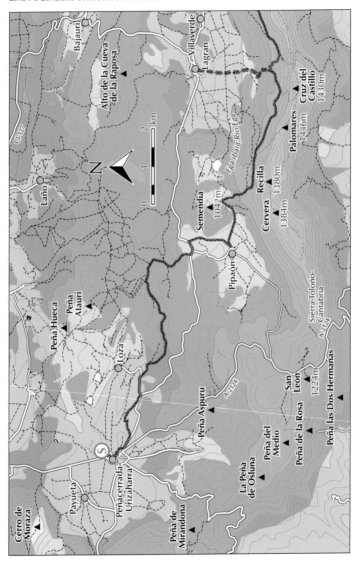

STAGE 2

Peñacerrada to Bernedo

Start	Bus stop on the main road east of Peñacerrada (740m)
Distance	24km
Ascent/Descent	870m/900m
Grade	3/4
Walking time	8hr 10min
Maximum altitude	1050m

An easy day's walk which, if the weather is kind, will provide excellent views of the Sierra Toloño, a ridge of jagged limestone mountains running west to east. The route runs through beech woods on the northern flank of a range that reaches 1446m (Palomares). Lunch should available at Lagran if the bar is open.

From the bus stop head south. Take the second left following a path that heads east out of the village and then south back to the main road. Continue east along the road leaving it after 600 metres. Head east across country and rejoin the road. Follow the road to the bottom of a valley and join a dirt road heading southeast near a stream.

Follow the dirt trail east for 300 metres and then southeast and east along the course of a stream through a valley for 3km. Turn south and join a road after 1.2km. Follow the road east for 500 metres ignoring the turn-off to the south, to pick up an agricultural trail into **Pipaón**.

> **Pipaón** is small village with no services (although a bar – Bar Pipaón – is listed on the council website), dominated by a large 16th-century church dedicated to the Exaltation of the Holy Cross. Inside the church is a Romanesque chapel.

Head out of the village the same way and turn east along a dirt road after about 100 metres. After another

Looking down to Villafría approaching Bernedo

800 metres start a steep 300-metre climb up into the Sierra Toloño. 2km from Pipaón the route starts to contour through a wonderful beech forest and continues east

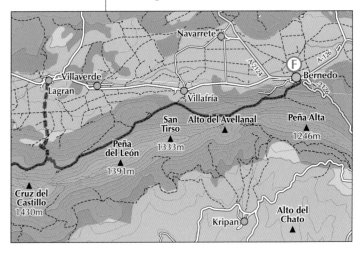

for 4km. ▶ After 4km the route joins up with the 'Wine and Fish Trail', the GR38, and a variant heads down to **Lagrán**.

> **Lagrán** is a small village north of the junction of the GR1 and the GR38. Fairly primitive accommodation is provided in a hostel (945 37 80 59, sheet sleeping bag needed) about a kilometre outside the village next to a chapel dedicated to San Bartolomé. The village plays host to a purpose-built GR38 interpretation centre with Restaurante La Traviesa (945 06 33 33) nearby and a bar, El Fronton Jatetxea, which does food.

The main route continues through beech forest, descending and then climbing 200 metres before a final descent down to **Bernedo**, 8km on from the junction with the GR38.

Watch out for information boards describing how the forest used to be used for the charcoal production.

BERNEDO POPULATION 545

Bernedo still has remnants of its defensive medieval walls, including the main gateway. The ruins of Castle Bernedo above the town are evidence of its importance in the Middle Ages when it was coveted by both kingdoms of Navarre and Castile. The size of the church dedicated to Our Lady of the Nativity also suggests it was fairly prosperous.

Bernedo has a range of services including a pleasant coffee bar near the church – the Bar Candi – and the Restaurant Arriete and cashpoints. Accommodation is available in the town at a casa rural, La Pikurutz (660 071 526, www.lapikurutza.com) or at the Golf Hotel Urturi (see www.booking.com) about 4km to north in the village of Urturi. The hotel will arrange transport to and from Bernedo.

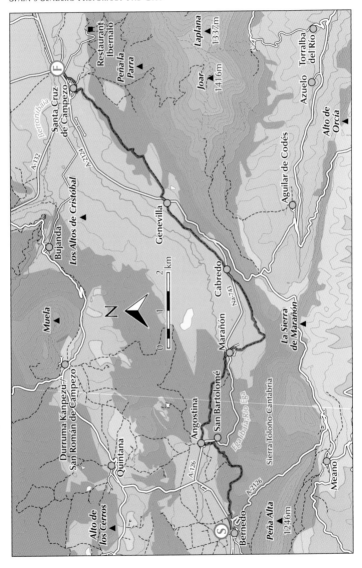

STAGE 3
Bernedo to Santa Cruz de Campezo

Start	Main road, northern side of Bernedo (720m)
Distance	19.5km
Ascent/Descent	510m/580m
Grade	3/4
Walking time	6hr 15min
Maximum altitude	800m

An easy walk that, after an initial climb, follows the southern edge of wide-open valley. A GR1 variant starting halfway along is marginally longer and not recommended. It should be possible to get to Santa Cruz de Campezo for a late lunch.

Join the main road on the northern side of Bernedo and follow it east, past the bus stop and the K39 marker, and take the first right along a smaller road that hairpins south up a hill. After 100 metres leave the road and follow a dirt track up through trees for 1.6km and arrive at a junction with another track, turn left and head north. After 300 metres (now descending), take a right fork and continue downhill for 1km towards a tiny chapel dedicated to **San Bartolomé** just off the route, and then continue north for another 300 metres into the tiny village of **Angostina**.

After Angostina the GR1 splits with a variant heading north out of the village. The recommended GR1 route follows a dirt road directly east across open fields. After 400 metres it turns south, heads into trees and reaches the top of a small hill after 300 metres. Stay on the dirt road and head southeast for 1km all the way to **Marañón**.

> **Marañón** is another tiny village. It has a bar, 'La Globa', and a pretty Romanesque church dedicated to Our Lady of the Assumption.

Ermita de Ibernalo

To get out of the village cross the bridge in the centre and head south past the church for 150 metres where the road swings right and, after another 200 metres, take a right-hand fork and head directly south. Follow a dirt road across open fields and climb gently south for 600 metres before turning east for 2km along a narrow tree-lined trail to the village of **Cabredo** (whose late Gothic church is dedicated to St James)

In the centre of village just past the church leave the main road and fork left to the cemetery. Then fork right to follow another tree-lined trail that starts on the southern side of the cemetery and continue northeast for 2km to the village of **Genevilla**.

Genevilla is another tiny village, its Gothic-Renaissance church, dedicated to Saint Stephan has a particularly important wooden altarpiece carved in the Flemish style.

Head east through Genevilla, turn left onto the main road and follow it for about 50 metres. Take an oblique right off the road and follow a side road that leads to the cemetery. Turn right at the cemetery and head southeast along a dirt road to the ruins of a chapel dedicated to Our Lady of Encinedo. 200 metres after the cemetery take a left fork in the dirt road and head northeast through an increasingly wooded landscape continuing for 5km to **Santa Cruz de Campezo**.

SANTA CRUZ DE CAMPEZO POPULATION 1100

Santa Cruz de Campezo was another town fought over by the Kingdoms of Navarre and Castille, losing its castle and defensive walls in the process. The most important building is the parish church dedicated to the Assumption of Our Lady, a building that has Romanesque, Gothic and Renaissance elements.

The town has a good range of services including cashpoints, bars and three restaurants. Accommodation can be found at the Restaurant Ibernalo, an annex to the Ermita de Ibernalo, a kilometre east of the town (945 102 271; **www.ibernalorural.com**).

To get to **Restaurant Ibernalo**, the only available accommodation for the night, walk east along the main street within the town (not the bypass running to the north) into the main square. Continue for 250 metres in the same direction out of the square, passing the church on its northern side, to where the road forks. Take the right fork and follow the road out of town for 1.5km. ▶

This road is not the 'official GR1' but provides a more straightforward way of getting to the only available accommodation.

STAGE 4
Santa Cruz de Campezo to Los Arcos

Start	Restaurant Ibernalo, Santa Cruz de Campezo (570m)
Distance	29km
Ascent/Descent	1070m/1250m
Grade	4/3
Walking time	10hr
Maximum altitude	1244m

Stage 4 is the toughest of the section but rewards with some amazing views, particularly when the Sierra de Codés is finally climbed and crossed. All the hard work is at the beginning and it's an easy walk to Los Arcos. If ten hours is too long then consider an overnight stop at the Santuario de Nuestra Señora de Codés where you can also get lunch if the restaurant is open.

From the restaurant take the road back south to the hairpin bend and picnic tables where there should be waymarks for the GR1. The route then leaves the road and climbs south up a valley and through a forest of huge evergreen oaks. After 400 metres and a climb of 100m, turn left and head east along a dirt road.

There is a variant that follows the Barranco La Dormida gorge and takes a more direct and much steeper climb to the top.

After 2km turn south and start to climb steeply, firstly zig-zagging and then heading west before turning a semi-circle and heading east. After 1.5km and another 300 metres of climb the route reaches the top, a lovely limestone ridge with amazing views particularly to the north. ◄

Follow a well-defined path west along the ridge. To the south, across a flat plateau, is a higher line of mountains, the **Sierra de Codés**. After 2.5km turn south, cross the plateau and head through a gap in the mountains (with **Joar** (1416m) to the west and **Laplana** (1337m) to the east). At the pass the views across the Ebro valley to the south and along cliffs to the east and west are stunning.

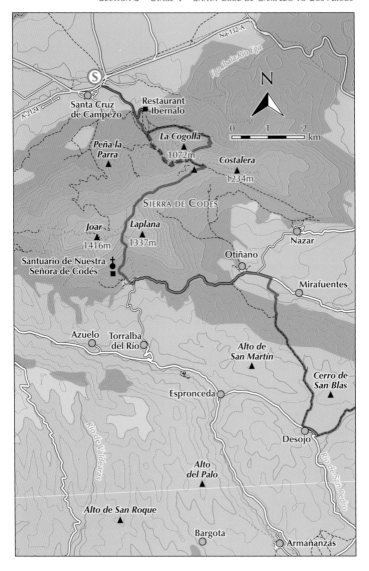

115

Santuario de Nuestra Señora de Codés.

From the pass the route descends south, dropping 400m over 1.5km, before reaching **Santuario de Nuestra Señora de Codés**.

The **Santuario** owes its location to the discovery in 1350, in a nearby cave, of an image of the Virgin and Child. The current building was constructed between the 16th and 18th century and includes an impressive baroque tower. The Santuario also provides food and accommodation (948 378 914; www.hospederiadecodes.com).

From the Santuario the route heads east along a road for 4km down to the tiny village of **Otiñano** that is dominated by a grand neo-classical house.

The route continues out of the village along a road heading east. The GR1 is now in arable countryside and the route across the field to the south seems to have disappeared. After walking along the road for about 700 metres an agricultural road on the other side of the field to the south should be visible. Cross the field, join the agricultural road and head east – the waymarks reappear.

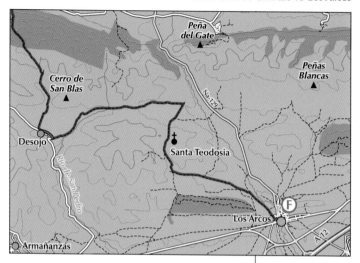

The route then heads south (the village of **Mirafuentes**, which the route doesn't go through, is about 200 metres to the east).

After turning south along a dirt road, continue for 500 metres to a low ridge, cross a junction with another dirt road and head from arable fields into a land of low trees and shrubs. Continue south, leave the dirt road, follow a path for 1.8km and join another dirt road. Follow the dirt road for 1.8km into the village of **Desojo**, which has a large church dedicated to Saint Mary with Gothic and Renaissance elements. There is a small community bar, the 'Balancín', which may be open.

Follow the road to the east of Desojo , leave it and head east along a dirt road. Ignore three right-hand exits and continue east and then north for 1km to meet a junction with two other dirt roads. Turning east continue for 3km (ignoring a right turn after 1.4km and a left turn shortly after) to a junction with another dirt road and head south. From the junction, and ignoring turns to the right and left, continue south and climb over a small ridge. ▶

To the left on top of the ridge is an isolated chapel dedicated to Santa Teodosia.

After 2km turn east onto another dirt trail and follow a valley for 3.5km down to **Los Arcos**. You should be able to see the town with its towers well before you arrive.

LOS ARCOS POPULATION 1167

Los Arcos is a milestone on the St James Way and from the Middle Ages onwards owed much of its prosperity to the pilgrims that streamed through it. It's also the first town the GR1 hits heading east through Navarre. Enter the town by the Portal de Castilla (Castilla – the neighbouring medieval kingdom) on the remnants of the city wall and into a lovely square, the Plaza Santa Maria, with a bar on the left-hand side and a huge elaborate arch to the door of the Santa Maria church on the right. It's the largest parish church in Navarre, built and rebuilt between the 12th and 19th centuries, and includes a wide range of architectural styles. Inside are a number of important artefacts. Particularly extravagant is a huge baroque altarpiece including a black Madonna with oriental features and blue eyes.

The town has the full range of services including restaurants, hotels and cash-points. There is a lot of hostel accommodation for the pilgrims but if you prefer a hotel then the Mónaco is good value (948 640 000; www.hotelmonaco.es) or the Pensión Ostadar (popular with pilgrims and on Booking.com).

STAGE 5
Los Arcos to Larraga

Start	Hotel Monaco, Los Arcos (450m)
Distance	39km; shortcut: 35km
Ascent/Descent	300m/350m
Grade	2/1
Walking time	10hr 40min; shortcut: 9hr 40min
Maximum altitude	470m

Stage 5 is long and monotonous but easy. The route is also hard to follow, particularly in the middle section where it travels through an agricultural landscape where paths are subject to change. The shortcut is recommended. For a late morning break stop at Allo.

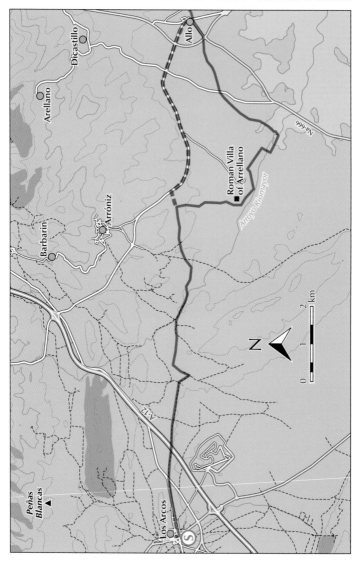

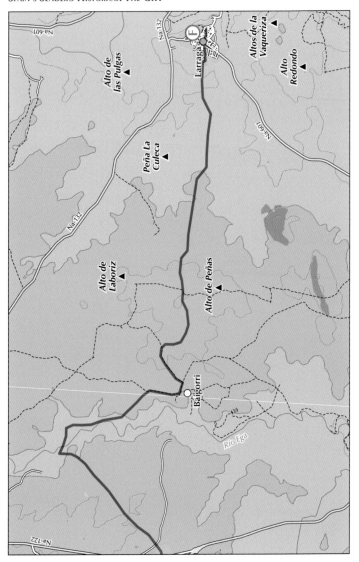

Leave the town along the Avenue Sancho el Sabio that runs along the southern side of the square near the hotel. After 1.6km cross a main road (the NA-110) and join a dirt road on the other side. Continue east for 700 metres and pass underneath a motorway (A-12) via a tunnel. Continue east along the same dirt road for 2km crossing two junctions with other roads running north–south.

After 2km take a left turn at a T-junction, head north for 500 metres to reach another junction, cross it and again head east. Ignoring turn-offs along dirt roads to the north and south continue east for another 4.5km before turning south. The south turn is the first of two leaving the dirt road before it reaches agricultural buildings set off on the dirt road's north side. ▶

For the next 9km the GR1 takes a roundabout route to the town of Allo. It can be a frustrating walk as farmers change the route.

Shortcut

If you are pressed for time then, instead of turning south near the agricultural buildings, continue east for another 600 metres until you reach a small road that you can follow all the way to town. This will shorten your walk by 4km.

The route follows the dirt road heading south for 2km before turning east. The original route may have been destroyed so head for a road about 400 metres to the east and a modern building covering the remains of the **Roman Villa of Arrellano**.

> Judging by its foundations, the **Roman Villa of Arrellano** (also known as the Roman Villa of the Muses) must have been huge, and its wine cellars and elaborate mosaics are an indication of how wealthy the area was in Roman times – see **www.guiartenavarra.com**.

On the road heading south from the Roman Villa there is a bridge over a stream. Leave the road just before bridge and head east. After 700 metres take the right-hand turn at a junction and head southeast along a dirt road. After 600 metres the route reaches a junction with

Allo is a small town with a range of services including a bar/restaurant – the Iraxoa.

another dirt road and turns right, heading southwest for 200 metres before crossing a bridge over a stream and turning left. Turn left after 400 metres and head northeast along a dirt road for 2km to cross a road, and carry on in an easterly direction for 2km to the town of **Allo**. ◄

In the centre of Allo turn right and head south down the main street (Paseo la Fuente) and turn left along Calle Nueva. At the end of Calle Nueva continue in the same direction along Calle la Balsa and follow this street to a car park and a road. Crossing the road the GR1 joins a dirt road.

For the next 4km follow a dirt road in a northeast direction. Heading gently downhill the route eventually reaches the **Río Ega**, crosses it by a bridge and heads southeast along a road. Follow the road for 400 metres and turn south along a dirt road following the river through vineyards. After 2.8km the route reaches the abandoned village of **Baigorri** complete with the dramatic ruins of a 12th-century castle and palace whose previous occupants included the Count of Lerin and the Duke of Alba.

The abandoned village of Baigorri

Turn right at Baigorri and head east for 300 metres before turning right again. Climb gently along a dirt road for 1.2km until reaching a junction and turning left. Continue climbing south and then east for 2km past turns to the right and left before starting a descent. Continue east for 7km to **Larraga**.

LARRAGA POPULATION 2152

Larraga sits on a hill in the middle of the Navarra plain overlooking the Río Arga. The town has a number of fine Baroque buildings, in particular the church of St Miguel with its enormous tower.

It has a good range of services, cashpoints and three hotels: the Hotel Villa de Larraga (948 711 246; www.villadelarraga.com), Hotel Rural el Castillo (948 711 778; www.hotelruralelcastillo.com) and the Hostal Casa Perico (948 711 152) all on www.booking.com.

STAGE 6
Larraga to Olite

Start	Church of St Miguel, Larraga (430m)
Distance	28km
Ascent/Descent	250m/250m
Grade	2/2
Walking time	7hr 40min
Maximum altitude	460m

Stage 6 is shorter than Stage 5 but in terms of walking is similar – another day across the fairly flat plain of northern Navarre with limited waymarks. For an early morning break stop at Berbinzana after which there is nothing until Olite.

From the church head southeast along the Carreterra Berbinzana and turn abruptly right off the main road

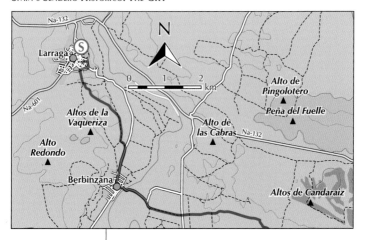

Below to the east is the Río Arga. ◄

(which swings east) and join the Calle el Huerto. Head west for a few metres and turn left and head south. The road turns quickly into an agricultural road and descends gently through fields and farms. ◄

Cross a junction after 300 metres and continue southeast. After 2km and a descent into the flat fields of the valley bottom, take the left turn at a fork and follow the trail to a road, turn right and head into the little town of **Berbinzana** some 4.5km from Larraga.

> **Berbinzana** is a small town on the western side of a Romanesque bridge over the Río Arga. There is a cashpoint and a bar – the Bar la Taberna.

Cross the bridge and follow the road east for 600 metres. Leave the road, which turns north, and follow an agricultural road (across flat and intensely farmed land) east for 1.1km before reaching a junction with another road.

Cross the road and continue east along a dirt road for 2km to a fork. Take the right fork and continue southeast for 1km. The route turns directly onto a *cañada real*

and follows it for the next 3.7km (crossing a road running west–east after 1.4km).

Cañada real a few kms after Berbinzana

> **Cañada real** are transhumance routes which were given a statutory basis in 1273 by Alfonso X (Alfonso the Wise). Often featured on maps, it is sometimes hard to spot them on the ground. They should have a width of 90 Castillian 'varas' (72.22m), are usually long (500km) and nearly always run north–south. They are an important feature of walking in Spain and have been included in the indicative list of Unesco sites.

2.3km after crossing the road leave the cañada real and turn east along an agricultural road. After 1.8km cross a junction, continue east for 1.4km to another junction, cross it and carry on for 200 metres. At this point the original path appears to have been destroyed so turn left and head northeast for 700 metres until the road reaches a junction, and then turn right and walk southeast for 700 metres (taking the left-hand fork at a junction after 300 metres) where the agricultural road turns east. If the going is dry than cut across the field and avoid the detour.

125

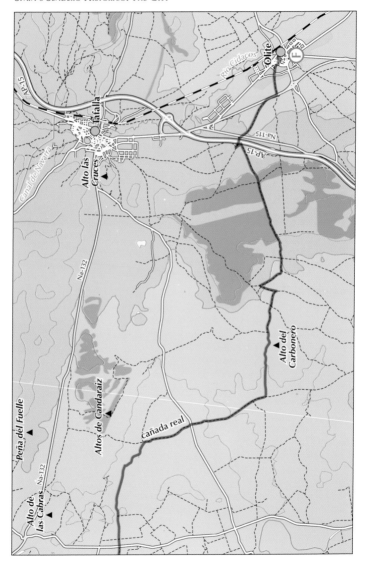

Head east up a gentle ascent for 1km arriving at a junction with a track heading south. Continue east along the edge of a forest along a level path. After 1.5km the path starts to descend and, emerging from the forest, presents views of Olite. The route follows the path down the hill, over a bridge across a motorway and through a tunnel under a smaller road. From the tunnel follow an agricultural road across fields southeast for a kilometre before going through another tunnel under a road and heading into **Olite**.

Olite

OLITE POPULATION 3832

Olite is a real gem. It was the royal headquarters of Navarre during the Middle Ages and is widely regarded as having some of the best Gothic architecture in Europe. With its city walls built on Roman foundations still intact, and its setting on a fairly flat plain, it bears comparison with Carcassonne in France. The dominant and most important building is the Palace of Kings that, with its turrets and towers, has all the ingredients of a fairytale castle albeit on an epic scale. Other important buildings include the church of San Pedro, the oldest church in Olite, and the church of Santa Maria La Real whose amazing archway surrounds the main entrance. If you have time then the Wine Museum is well worth a visit.

Situated in a lovely 17th-century building, a former palace, each floor is dedicated to a separate stage in the wine-making process.

If you need it, Olite is one of the best places on the GR1 to get pampered – there are a number of upmarket hotels including a Parador in the 'Old Palace' – a converted wing of the Palace of Kings. For a more economical option try the Hotel Garcia Ramirez (**www.hotelgarciaramirez.com** and **www.booking.com**).

4 OLITE TO MURILLO DE GÁLLEGO

The Norman tower at Biel

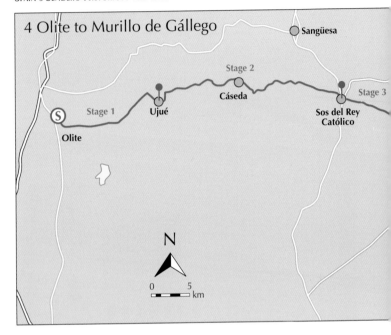

4 Olite to Murillo de Gállego

Sangüesa

Stage 2

Cáseda

Stage 3

Ujué

Sos del Rey
Católico

Stage 1

Olite

N

0   5 km

The middle section of the route is short but spectacular with the GR1 crossing lovely landscapes and visiting a series of dramatic historical sites.

It takes half a day's walking from Olite to escape the flat plain of northern Navarre and climb up into the Sierra de Ujué for the first taste of Pyrenean foothills (or the Prepirineo as they are called in Spain). The mountains are not high (less than 1000m) but high enough to provide some excellent views, including views of the Pyrenees themselves. The most spectacular scenery is reached at the Mallos de Riglos and Mallos de Agüero where the huge

red cliffs are a mecca for climbers from all over the world.

Although the landscape is excellent it's the towns and villages along the route that really stand out. The most famous is Sos del Rey Católico, birthplace of Ferdinand whose marriage to Isabella effectively unified Spain, but Ujué, Biel, Gallipienzo Antiguo and Agüero all compete.

In this and for the rest of the GR1 the presence of the old 'border' with Moorish Spain becomes evident. The main evidence is a series of castles and watchtowers often in stunning locations built in a line by Sancho Garces

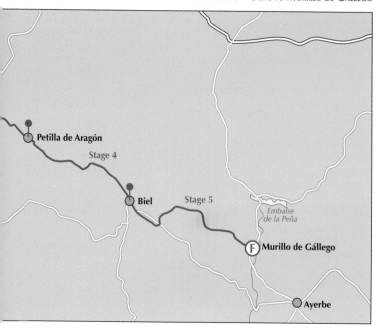

I, King of Navarre (Pamplona) between 905 and 925 to protect his part of the Marche Hispáncia from Moorish Spain (the Umayyad Caliphate). Sometimes built on the remains of captured Moorish buildings they were usually positioned to command the head of a valley and, as well as keeping out the Moors, served a similar function against rivals from Castille.

Sancho was grandfather of Sancho the Great (992–1035), the most important of all the Sanchos. In the face of the fragmentation of Moorish Spain he began a policy of expansion and, as a precursor to Ferdinand and Isabella, succeeded in unifying all the kingdoms of Christian Spain (only to split his inheritance between his three sons thereby delaying eventual unification by nearly 300 years). He was hugely successful and influential and his power extended into southwest France as well as across northern Spain. Of interest to walkers at the time was his improvement of the road from Cluny to León along which pilgrims flocked on their way to Santiago de Campostela – as such Sancho was one of the original sponsors of the St James Way.

ACCESS AND ACCOMMODATION

The section is broken into five stages and the boundary from Navarre to Aragón is crossed on the third stage. Waymarking improves significantly in Aragón although once in the mountains the route is easy to follow in Navarre as well.

From Riglos, near Murillo de Gállego, you can catch an early morning train to Zaragoza and its international airport, or continue by train to Madrid, or catch a taxi to Ayerbe and, from there catch a bus to Huesca and Zaragoza.

Accommodation is available all along the route although it is limited to a casa rural in Ujué and a hostel or casa rural in Biel. Sos del Rey Católico has a parador if pampering is required and you can also treat yourself to a spa hotel in Murillo de Gállego (featuring a dining room with amazing views of the Mallos de Riglos).

SECTION 4: KEY INFORMATION	
Distance	110km
Total ascent	4020m
Total descent	3860m
Alternative schedule	If time is available consider staying at Sos del Rey Católico where there is so much to see. If you're on a tight budget, stay at Riglos instead of Murillo de Gállego.

STAGE 1
Olite to Ujué

Start	Royal Palace, Olite (385m)
Distance	16km
Ascent/Descent	540m/170m
Grade	3/3
Walking time	5hr
Maximum altitude	838m

Stage 1 is a short easy walk and completes the traverse of the plain of northern Navarre. Aim to get to Ujué at about 3pm and enjoy a late lunch at the lovely Meson las Torres. The casa rurals at Ujué don't do dinner so the alternative would be a very late meal in one of the restaurants.

Leave through the main gate on Olite's eastern side next to the palace. Cross the road running at right angles to the gate and head east along the Avenue San Martín de Unx. At end of the avenue walk through the underpass underneath the railway line and continue east for about 400 metres, cross a bridge over a river and follow a path going south beside the river. After 200 metres the path crosses a road, joins an agricultural road and continues in the same direction for another 600 metres to a junction with another similar road.

On the flat agricultural plain the church that dominates **Ujué** should be visible on the eastern horizon. There are also fine views back to Olite.

Continue east past pig farms and vineyards. After 1.3km cross an agricultural road running north south and 600 metres later, take a left turn along another agricultural road. After 1.1km cross through a gap in a low

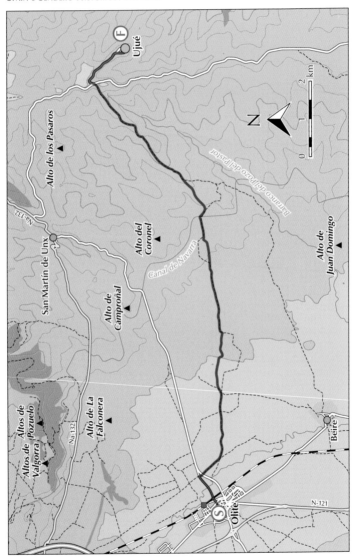

The Canal de Navarra

uncultivated ridge before continuing east for another 600 metres to the **Canal de Navarra**.

> The 177km **Canal de Navarra**, completed in 2014 after several years, carries water for irrigation from the north of Navarre to the south. The canal's construction was controversial and opposed by environmentalists.

Continue east, climbing gradually for 2.2km before joining a dirt road coming up from the south. Head northeast for 200 metres, turn right and head east again. Continue in the same direction for another kilometre ignoring dirt roads from the north and south before leaving the road and following a path through gorse and shrub northeast for a further kilometre.

After rejoining a dirt road the route continues, firstly on the south and then the north side of a ridge for 2.2km before joining a road and heading into **Ujué**. The views of Ujué from the junction are excellent and it's one of the best places to get a picture.

UJUÉ POPULATION 198

Ujué is a medieval hilltop town with the church of Santa Maria (a national monument) its crowning glory. It's a real beauty spot. The town was originally built as a defence against the Moors but then declined in significance until its potential was spotted during the heyday of the kingdom of Navarre. The church includes both Romanesque (11th century) and Gothic elements (15th century) and includes some wonderful Gothic decorations on the facade. Of particular importance inside is the image of the Virgin of Ujué, made of wood in 1190 and further embellished in the 15th century. The statue acknowledges the legend of a shepherd who was attracted to a hole by doves, only to find an image of Santa Maria there. Ujué became a pilgrimage destination thereafter.

There are three restaurants – the Meson Las Torres, the Asador Uxue and Los Migos. The Meson Las Torres has the best location. Rooms are available at two casa rurales – at the Isolina Jurio (948 739 037) and El Chofer (948 739 011). El Chofer serves an excellent breakfast. It is to be found on the Ctra San Martin, the most westerly street in the town.

STAGE 2
Ujué to Sos del Rey Católico

Start	Ruined church of San Miguel, Ujué (838m)
Distance	34km
Ascent/Descent	860m/1010m
Grade	3/4
Walking time	10hr 50min
Maximum altitude	838m

Stage 2 is a long but very rewarding walk with a varied landscape and interesting towns. Sos del Rey Católico, the destination, is one of the highlights of the GR1. There is no accommodation on the route and a taxi from Cáseda to Sangüesa (11km journey) is the best way to break the stage if you need to.

Leave along a dirt road to the left-hand side of the church. Follow it east steeply down the side of a valley before turning left 600 metres from the ruined church. Continue down into the valley (heading west) for 600 metres turning east again at the bottom. Cross a bridge over a stream and continue east, contouring round into another valley, crossing a bridge over another stream after 800 metres. After continuing east up the side of the valley for 200 metres, turn west and then north reaching the top of a ridge after 600 metres.

Crossing the ridge the route enters a long valley running from west to east. Follow the dirt road north across the head of the valley for 500 metres and then east as it zig-zags down the valley for 3.8km. The route follows the dirt road round to the north, crosses a small valley and then starts to climb east. After 500 metres it passes a low stone single barn before turning north 100 metres later. After a gentle descent it starts to climb again to the east, then northeast, before levelling out after 1.3km.

To the east the church above **Gallipienzo Antiguo** should be visible. Go to the church, descend into the

Gallipienzo Antiguo

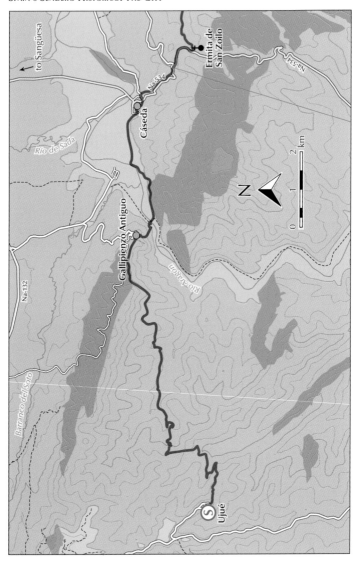

churchyard on its right-hand side by some wooden steps, pass through it, and head down into the village.

Gallipienzo Antiguo is a wonderful, slightly eerie place located high on the side of a gorge above the Río Aragón. A significant town at the turn of the 19th century its population is now ten per cent of what it was and abandoned houses and farms litter the hillside. The village has two churches both with Gothic and Romanesque elements. One, passed on the way in, is dedicated to the Saviour and other in town is dedicated to San Pedro. There are also the ruins of a castle.

The route heads down through the village, leaves on its southern side and then passes down through ruined terraces to a bridge over the river. The precise route is hard to follow but if you end up on the riverside dirt road then follow it north under the bridge where another dirt road will lead you back up onto the bridge.

Cross the bridge and follow the trail up the hill, turning left after 50 metres and continuing for 1.8km along the dirt trail running parallel with the **Río Aragón**. The route then turns east and heads though fields for 1.6km to the town of **Cáseda**.

Like Gallipienzo Antiguo, **Cáseda** sits on a hill next to the Río Aragón. Although not in such a dramatic location it has managed to hold onto its population and has shops, a bakery and a bar/restaurant (Imperio).

If you need to break this stage, a taxi from Cáseda to Sangüesa (11km journey) is the best option. **Sangüesa** is an interesting town in its own right and has plenty of accommodation (for example, www.hotelyamaguchi.com).

Finding the route out of Cáseda is a bit of a challenge. The route follows a valley out from the southeast and to get to it walk through the middle of the town

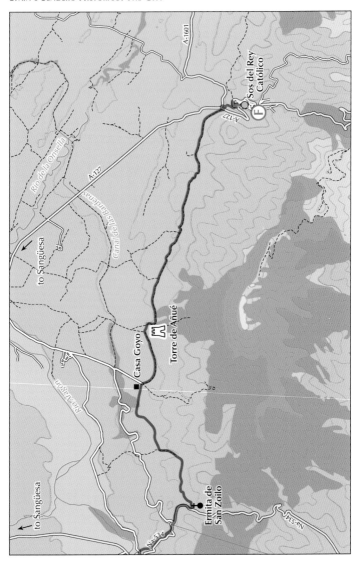

along the main high street (past the bar/restaurant Imperio), turn left and head down the hill, cross the main road (bakery on the left) and continue down along a road to the edge of the town. As the road starts to turn northeast, a path with a waymark points to the south and along the valley. Follow the path south and then east along the valley joining a road after 1.2km. After following the road for a kilometre the route arrives at the **Ermita de San Zoilo**.

> This **chapel** is a pilgrimage destination and was an important stopover point for shepherds taking their flocks to and from pastures in the Pyrenees.

From the chapel take the dirt road north and then east crossing a junction with another dirt road after 1.4km. Continue north along the dirt road for another kilometre before turning east. The dirt road has now turned into a path and after 700 metres, unless it has been cleared, becomes overgrown and difficult to follow. The route continues east for about 100 metres and then turns to the northeast along the side of a field, turning east again after 600 metres.

After 800 metres, cross a road and continue east past a farmstead, the **Casa Goyo**, for another 2km. The dirt road then turns north. The route passes the **Torre de Añué**, the remains of a castle, 300 metres to the east across a field. The original path has been lost to agriculture and if it's wet this field could be very muddy. A detour north along a dirt road and back south again may be necessary.

From the Torre de Añué follow the dirt road south for 200 metres and turn east. Continue on this trail east for 7.7km, turning south for the last kilometre emerging onto the road just north of Sos del Rey Católico.

Turn left onto the road and head down the hill; turn right at the junction and cross a bridge. Once over the bridge waymarks point the way directly along a path up a steep hill, onto a road and into **Sos del Rey Católico**.

SOS DEL REY CATÓLICO POPULATION 629

Sos del Rey Católico is a wonderful place. Originally named Sos the town was granted the additional 'del Rey Católico' in 1925 in recognition of the fact that it is the birthplace of Fernando II who, with Isabella, unified the kingdoms of Aragón, Navarre and Castile – a key moment in Spanish history. Ironically, by unifying the three kingdoms, Ferdinand undermined the significance of Sos as a strategic border town. It had owed its development to its physical and political location. Its location on a promontory made it easy to fortify and the benefits of this were recognised even before the arrival of the Romans. Occupied by the Moors, it became a border town firstly between the Moors and the new kingdom of Navarre, then between Navarre and Aragón, and then finally between Navarre and Castile.

Inside the town, behind the defensive walls, everything is tightly packed and claustrophobic and finding your way through the tiny streets and towering buildings is a challenge. There is a lot to see if you can find it. Highlights include the church of San Esteban, a Romanesque church built in the 11th century and located at the top of the town; next to it the castle with its tower, originally built by Moors in 975; below it, a sort of crypt, the Church of St Mary of Forgiveness; the old market – La Lonja Medieval – another Romanesque building which also housed the medieval town council; the Sada Palace, where Ferdinand was born and which features an excellent Spanish heritage room; and nearby, the Church of St Martin of Tours situated on a rocky outcrop in the southern part of town and featuring original frescoes.

As you would expect at such an important tourist destination there is a lot of accommodation with options ranging from a youth hostel (948 888 480) through to the Parador Ferdinand of Aragón (948 888 017). The Hostal Las Coronas, located right in the middle next to the medieval market can be recommended. Its helpful owner is appropriately named Fernando (948 88 84 08; **www.hostallascoronas.com** and **www.booking.com**).

STAGE 3

Sos del Rey Católico to
Petilla de Aragón

Start	Parador Ferdinand of Aragón, Sos del Rey Católico (651m)
Distance	14km
Ascent/Descent	570m/360m
Grade	3/4
Walking time	4hr 50min
Maximum altitude	882m

Stage 3 is short and easy. You could combine it with the next stage but it would turn two easy stages into a long, hard one. The second part of the walk follows a path through trees.

The route leaves the town close to where it entered at its northern edge over the road beyond the parador. Follow the road past the parador to the main road and a GR1 signpost. Waymarks point the way along a path down the hill towards the **Monasterio de Valentuñana**. After 600 metres join a dirt road, turn right and head southeast and then east for 4.4km.

As the dirt road turns south, leave it and follow waymarks east across rough grazing and gorse. There are lots of animal trails and finding the path is difficult, but the route heads east (slightly to the south of east) until after 500 metres it reaches trees, a high fence and a gate with a waymark on its right-hand post.

Pass through the gate into the trees and follow a well-defined path east-southeast for 2.5km to a small road. After following the road for 50 metres continue east as the road turns south. Once again the route is following a forest path.

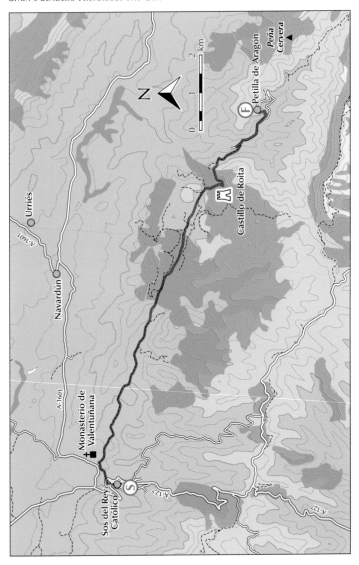

Looking over Sos

After 400 metres or so waymarks offer a detour up to the **Castillo de Roita**, the ruins of a hill-top castle built on the remains of a Moorish castle captured in the 10th century and rebuilt in the 11th.

The route is now passing through a lovely forest of pine and beech. A kilometre from the junction with the road and after climbing steadily, turn south and descend around the head of a valley crossing a stream near a waterfall at the bottom. ▶

From the path on the other side there are views of the Castillo de Roita.

Follow the path up from the stream reaching the next ridge after 500 metres and then descend through trees into the next valley. After 200 metres join a dirt trail and follow it southeast down to a road. Take the road south for a kilometre until waymarks point to a path on the left-hand side into the village of **Petilla de Aragón**.

PETILLA DE ARAGÓN POPULATION 35

Petilla de Aragón is in one of two tiny enclaves of Navarre entirely surrounded by the region of Aragón. Its distinct status dates back to the Middle Ages and the settlement of a debt between the two kingdoms. A pretty hilltop village, it is the birthplace of the Nobel Laureate Santiago Ramón y Cajal, widely regarded as the founder of modern neuroscience.

The Hostal Santiago Ramón y Cajal is near the trail as you enter the village (948 925 060).

145

STAGE 4
Petilla de Aragón to Biel

Start	Village square, Petilla de Aragón (860m)
Distance	21km
Ascent/Descent	1010m/1050m
Grade	4/4
Walking time	7hr 50min
Maximum altitude	1132m

Another wonderful and very remote forest walk, with an optional hill climb, that, on a good day, can offer great views of the Pyrenees. There is a place for a swim but nowhere to get food.

Follow the main village road out and round the head of a valley. After 200 metres turn left onto a dirt road and follow it east past a chapel dedicated to the **Virgin de Caridad** and down the side of the valley before turning south. Continue along the path in a south-southeasterly direction for a kilometre before joining a dirt road (although it is initially unclear whether the route runs along the dirt road or the path on the other side of a fence). Continue east for another 1.2km and join up with a dirt road from the west and carry on east.

After 200 metres ignore a turn-off to the north and head southeast climbing all the time with a couple of zig-zags for 1.6km to a junction with another dirt road joining from the west. Continue east until a pass is reached after 700 metres and cross into a more open valley.

Once over the pass (and into the autonomous region of Aragón) follow a path on the southern side of a valley along the boundary between grazing land and trees and head southeast for 1.6km. The route then enters another valley with grazing in the bottom and heads east. After 900 metres it arrives at the stunning

twin towers of the **Castillo de Sibirana** and the Chapel de Santa Quiteria.

Castillo de Sibirana

> The **Castillo de Sibirana** was built in the early 10th century by Sancho Garces I and includes elements from an earlier one built by the Moors dating back to the mid-9th century.

Continue past the castle and southeast for 3km along a pretty valley through patches of grazing. Reaching a concrete road and a bridge over a **stream**, turn left and northeast following the stream up a valley towards a campsite.

> This is a popular beauty spot in the summer and, if the weather is good, this is the spot for a **swim**. There are also signs to a **mountain refuge** should it be needed.

Continue on past the campsite and follow a dirt road that zig-zags its way up the hill. After 400 metres leave it and follow a path climbing southeast steeply up

147

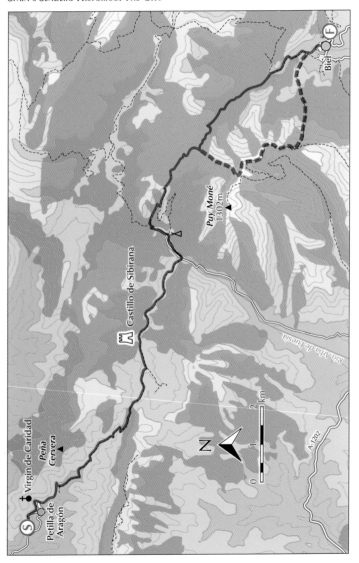

through trees. After 900 metres the route joins a dirt road and continues to climb southeast for another 400 metres where it leaves the road and continues on a path for 1.8km before reaching a pass. The total climb from the campsite is about 300m.

From the ridge there are two routes down to Biel.

Scenic extension (4km)

The more scenic route continues south along the ridge for 1.5km, where you can either turn west and do a return trip to the top of **Puy Moné** (1302m) or turn east and descend down to a path that turns south and then east for 5km into Biel. Views of the Pyrenees from the top are excellent.

To take the more direct route, carry on along the ridge, cross it and head southeast along a well-defined trail down a wooded hillside and into a valley. After 3km the track levels out and drops into a flat-bottomed valley and follows it, after crossing a bridge, into **Biel**.

BIEL POPULATION 157

Biel is a small town located next to the Río Arba. It is dominated by a huge Romanesque tower, part of the castle of Biel and integrated with the church which was built with the help of Norman architects.

Accommodation is available in the hostel owned by the village – a bit primitive but clean and very cheap (976 669 001). A sheet sleeping bag is needed at the hostel and although there are cooking facilities there is no food. The town also has a number of casa rurals the best organised of which is Apartmentos Las Lezas (695 406 000, **www.laslezas.com**). There is a restaurant and a bar in town but they are not open every night (Restaurant El Caserio 976 669 083).

STAGE 5
Biel to Murillo de Gállego

Start	Village centre, Biel (750m)
Distance	25km
Ascent/Descent	1030m/1320m
Grade	3/4
Walking time	9hr
Maximum altitude	970m

The last stage of the section is another remote, lonely one featuring some really dramatic scenery along the last stretch. Agüero, which comes 4km before you reach the end of the walk, has a bar and accommodation.

Follow the main road east out of Biel leaving it on the edge of the village to join a waymarked path heading east and then south across a low pass and back onto the road. Follow the road east leaving it on its south side after 100 metres. The route attempts to follow a path down into a little valley which can be very overgrown, and unless it's been cleared it's best to stay on the road which tracks around the valley to rejoin the route immediately south of a small farmstead (**Corral de Pelegrín**).

From the farmstead follow the dirt road southeast for 800 metres descending gently. The dirt road turns into a path which the route then follows, in the same direction, up through trees for 300 metres where it joins another dirt road. Follow this southeast for 200 metres before once again joining a path. Climbing gently continue southeast for the next 500 metres, following the course of some electric cables, up to a small road.

Cross the road, continue east (not the route of the electric cables) and down towards, but not onto, a road. Follow a path below and to the south of the road down to a stream and a small irrigation reservoir. Just past the

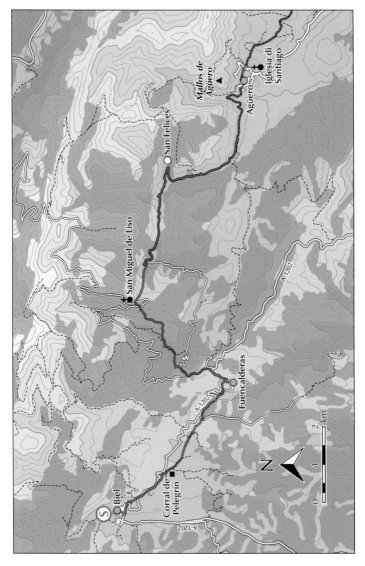

reservoir climb onto a concrete road, turn right and follow a walled path into the small village of **Fuencalderas**.

Leave Fuencalderas along the road heading north. After 500 metres, as the road swings to the east continue north along a path. After 150 metres join a dirt road and follow it north for 700 metres before taking a turn onto another dirt road heading east. 300 metres later leave the dirt road and head into trees along a path. Initially the path heads north but then turns east and descends steeply into a valley reaching a stream after 700 metres.

Cross the stream and follow a path northeast along the right-hand bank for about 400 metres before turning east and climbing up to a wooded ridge. On the far side of the ridge turn north and then northeast up an increasingly steep path for 900 metres, passing some ruined farm buildings before reaching a dirt trail. Cross the dirt trail and continue northeast for another 400 metres reaching open ground and a beautiful Romanesque chapel dedicated to **San Miguel de Liso**. ◀

With its defensive tower it belongs to the line of fortifications built by Sancho Garces I in the early 10th century.

From the pass turn east and downhill across open ground towards derelict farm buildings about 300 metres away. There are waymarks but on the open ground the path is difficult to spot. The route drops into an increasingly beautiful valley. Watch for waterfalls to the north. 900 metres from the pass and after crossing a stream the route joins a dirt road which it follows east for 3km to the village of **San Felices**.

> **San Felices** is a tiny village, almost abandoned. On the side of one of the houses is a huge conical chimney – part of a traditional Aragónese oven, a 'catiera' entered from the inside of the house.

The official GR1 then slavishly follows a dirt trail east out of the village before meandering back again – a detour of about 1km. It might be possible to avoid the detour by cutting down across a field but there are brambles guarding the way. The route then follows the dirt road south then east for 3.8km before reaching a fork.

At the fork, or just before it, the **views** open up: firstly Agüero and then, and after a few more metres, Agüero with the huge red cliffs of the Mallos de Agüero towering above. This is a stunning location an very much the place to take a picture.

Agüero

Take the left fork and follow the path down and round the valley, underneath the Peña Salinero (densely packed with huge Griffon vultures) and up into **Agüero**.

AGÜERO POPULATION 150

Agüero's dramatic location is not its only attraction. About 700 metres to the southeast is an incomplete church dedicated to **Santiago** which is a national monument and regarded as one of the gems of Romanesque architecture. Particularly impressive are the detailed sculptures around the main door and on the capitals. Agüero itself dates back to the Reconquista and is densely packed with steeply rising streets.

Accommodation can be found at the Hostal la Costera (974 380 330) and Casa Camilo (974 380 121) and there is a bar hidden away south of the church whose owner can be persuaded to make a wonderful *bocadillo*.

From the square in front of the church follow the Calle de Fuente to the edge of the village to a dirt trail and then

153

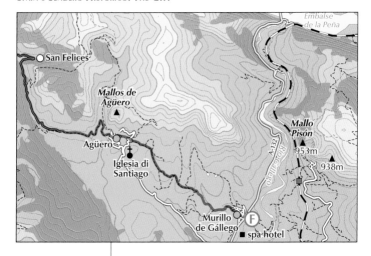

continue east across a shallow valley to a road. There is now an abundance of waymarks with GR1 signs competing for attention with smart new signs pointing the way on the Camino Natural Hoya de Huesca. Follow these and they will lead you the 4km to **Murillo de Gállego**.

MURILLO DE GÁLLEGO POPULATION 183

Murillo de Gállego sits at the point where the Río Gállego emerges through a gorge in the wall of red cliffs. Although most former residents have left, opportunities for rafting and other river activities now make it an important tourist destination and there are a several upmarket hotels. A huge church dedicated to San Salvador dominates the town. At its southern end it is Romanesque and rounded while at the other end, facing the town, it is Gothic and square. The semi-circular south facing flanks seem to mirror the buttress in the cliffs behind.

There are three hotels – the Los Mallos group (which has a hotel and an albergue) (www.panoramicalosmallos.com); the new spa hotel just to the south of town (www.hotelaguasdelosmallos.com and www.booking.com) and an upmarket central hotel, the Real Posada de Liena (www.realposadadeliena.com and www.booking.com). The spa hotel can be recommended not least because of its amazing views from the restaurant, although the rates, which are currently competitive, could go up once the new hotel becomes established.

5 MURILLO DE GÁLLEGO TO GRAUS

The high Pyrenees from Nazare

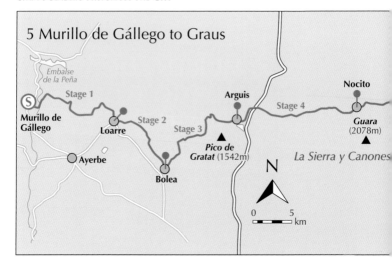

5 Murillo de Gállego to Graus

This section of the GR1 is special and guaranteed to leave a lasting impression. The scenery is incredible, the history is laid on with a trowel, but the real and unforgettable surprise is the multitude of abandoned villages. Populated until the late sixties and more concentrated here than anywhere else on the route, they retain a spooky freshness. Trust me, you can still hear the voices of the people who left in such a hurry.

The landscape is particularly interesting. The previous section offered a taster of the Mallos de Riglos; this one provides the full meal, visits Riglos itself and gets right underneath the fabulous red cliffs. Other highlights include the Parque Natural de la Sierra y Cañones de Guara dominated by the Tozal de Guara (2078m)

and a top European destination for the sport of canyoning.

As well as the immediate scenery the long-distance views are also excellent, particularly to the north and into the Pyrenees with views of Monte Perdido (3355m), Peña Montañesa (2295m), Cotiella (2912m) and Turbón (2492m).

Buildings marking the Marche Hispáncia border continue to show their presences with Loarre Castle, widely regarded as the best preserved Romanesque castle in the world, the highlight.

ACCESS AND ACCOMMODATION

This stretch of the GR1 would be ideal for a two-week holiday. To get

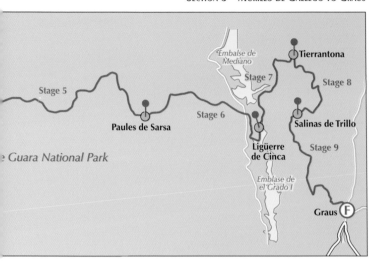

to Murillo de Gállego (or Riglos) fly to Madrid and take the train to Zaragoza or fly directly to Zaragoza. From Zaragoza take the morning train to Riglos (a short walk from Murillo de Gállego) or a bus from Huesca/Zaragoza (www.avanzabus.com) and stay in one of the hotels listed in the previous section. There is a direct train connection to and from Graus but there is also a good bus service with frequent connections to Zaragoza and on into the mainline train network. For times go to http://alosa.avanzabus.com.

Accommodation is generally plentiful and there are alternative ways of breaking up the trip if you want to take a more leisurely pace. The exception to this is the two days spent traversing the Parque Natural de la Sierra y Cañones de Guara. The second day is a tough one and to avoid a long tedious road walk at the end it is necessary to organise a lift with the casa rural (booking ahead essential). None of the accommodation listed involves leaving the route.

For most of its journey from Murillo de Gállego to Nocito, the GR1 mirrors a new and well-way-marked route – 'El Camino Natural de la Comarca de Hoya de Huesca'. There are three important exceptions and, risking the wrath of purists, the recommended route is based on the new route rather than the GR1. The new route, which at the beginning benefits from a €800,000 investment in a footbridge, is better and avoids two stretches of road that would otherwise spoil a near-perfect walk.

SECTION 5: KEY INFORMATION	
Distance	187.5km
Total ascent	7380m
Total descent	6970m
Alternative schedule	Nocito is a great place to stop for an extra day, with lots of excellent local walks and in particular a circular hike up to the top of Tozal de Guara the highest mountain in the Parque Natural de la Sierra y Cañones de Guara. You could also consider splitting Stage 5 into two by stopping at Rodellar (see Note at the start of the stage).

Loarre Castle (Stage 1)

STAGE 1
Murillo de Gállego to Loarre

Start	Main road east of Murillo de Gállego (542m)
Distance	19km
Ascent/Descent	1320m/1060m
Grade	5/5
Walking time	7hr 10min
Maximum altitude	1050m

This is a spectacular day's walking. It starts with a close inspection of the red Mallos de Riglos cliffs and finishes with the Loarre Castle. Weather permitting there will be views of both the Pyrenees and the Hoya de Huesca. Aim to get to Loarre for a late lunch although an early morning break at Riglos is also recommended.

Take the first left off the main road east of Murillo de Gállego (just past the Rafting and Adventure Centre) and follow the El Camino Natural de la Comarca de Hoya de Huesca (El Camino) signs east underneath a large power line, past a campsite and down to the new footbridge over the **Río Gállego**. The footbridge is 1.1km from the town and after crossing it GR1 waymarks reappear.

The route turns left and heads north joining a dirt road after 600 metres. It follows this north-northeast to **Riglos** (crossing a railway line after 1.1km) and reaches the village after 1.7km.

> **Riglos** is a tiny village nestling underneath 300m cliffs. It's an amazing location and very popular with climbers. There is accommodation (and a bar/restaurant) at a hostel, the Refugio de Riglos (**www. refugioderiglos.es**).

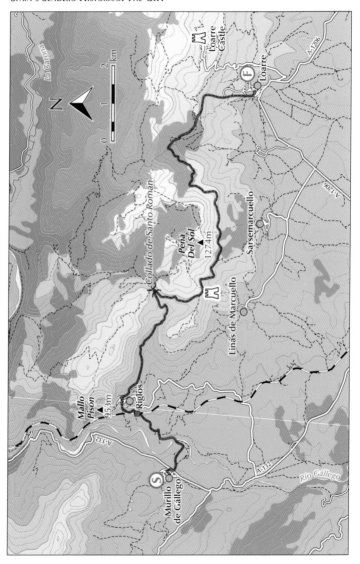

The scenery for the next 4km is spectacular and you will share it, almost certainly, with the vultures that live in massive cliffs above.

The village of Riglos under El Puro

From Riglos head southeast, parallel with the cliffs, along a dirt trail. Initially the cliffs are on the north side only but after 2km the route enters a gorge. After 3km the track becomes a path and, after 300 metres, turns north and climbs gently to the top of the **pass** with views of the Pyrenees.

At the top turn south (there is a junction with the GR95) and continue along a dirt road for 1.8km to the ruins of the Ermita de San Miguel and the **Torre de Marcuello**.

These **ruins** are another part of Sancho Garces I's defensive chain and, perched on the edge of the ridge are perhaps its most dramatic feature.

Torre de Marcuello and the Ermita de San Miguel

From the ruins the GR1 splits with El Camino. The GR1 heads down through the ruins to the village of **Linás de Marcuello**, and then east to **Sarsemarcuello**, and on in the same direction to the village of Loarre. El Camino stays high, sustains the wonderful views south across Huesca, and provides great views of Loarre Castle.

Following El Camino, continue along the dirt road east for 1.4km before taking a left turn and heading east along another dirt road. Follow the dirt road for 6km, leaving (to follow a path) and rejoining it just before heading south into the village of **Loarre**.

Loarre Castle is not actually on the trail but about 1.5km to the northeast of the village. It has to be visited. Built in the 11th century on the remains of old Roman walls, Loarre Castle was key to Sancho Garcia III's (one of Sancho the Great's sons) reconquest of Huesca. It's a perfect castle with towers to climb, arched bridges to cross and dungeons to investigate all amid a maze of corridors and tunnels. It is dominated by a pair of linked towers that provide fantastic views to the south.

The ornate Gothic windows are a highlight of the Torre de la Reina (Queen's tower). The penultimate floor of the Torre del Homenaje has a huge stone fireplace. The church of San Pedro was added to the castle in 1071. Ridley Scott used Loarre castle as a location for his 2003 film *Kingdom of Heaven*.

Accommodation is available in Loarre at the comfortable Hospederia de Aragón Loarre (974 382 706; www.hospederiadeloarre.com and www.booking.com) and in various casa rurals including: Casa El Callejón de Andresé (974 382 735; www.elcallejondeandrese.com and www.booking.com); Casa Pepico (974 382 616; www.casapepico.com). The village also has two bars/restaurants and a cashpoint machine.

STAGE 2

Loarre to Bolea

Start	Main square, Loarre (770m)
Distance	11km
Ascent/Descent	140m/270m
Grade	4/4
Walking time	3hr 15min
Maximum altitude	840m

At a push the next two stages could be combined. With the Loarre Castle and Bolea there is, however, plenty to see and given the tougher walking ahead it's a good chance to take it easy.

Leave from the northeast corner of the square to head through back streets to the eastern side of the village and a road. Follow the road north and then east over a bridge and out of the village. Head across a shallow valley and

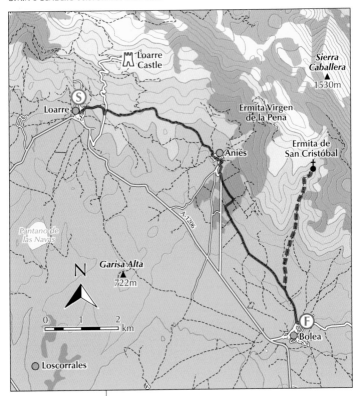

follow what is now a dirt path for about 700 metres before meeting the road heading up to **Loarre Castle**.

For walkers wanting to visit Loarre Castle on the same day as this short stage to Bolea, there is a higher traverse to the small shrine of the Ermita Virgen de la Peña, built into cliffs, and an easy descent to Aniés.

Cross the road and join a dirt trail following El Camino signs for 4km to **Aniés**. The GR1 takes a slightly

lower route and El Camino joins it just before entering the village.

Almond trees and Loarre Castle

Aniés is a small village with no services. The large parish church dedicated to St Stephen has Romanesque origins but was heavily remodelled in the 18th century.

▶ Cross Aniés and leave the village on its southern side following a path that runs almost parallel to the road. Join the road to cross a bridge about 600 metres south of the village. 100 metres after the bridge leave the road, turn left along a dirt trail and continue southeast for 700 metres before turning right (easily missed) onto a path through trees. There is a good view to the left of the red rock of the **Ermita Virgen de la Peña**. After 200 metres turn left onto another dirt road and follow it southeast for 4km to **Bolea**.

The GR1 and El Camino take slightly different routes from Aniés to Bolea and, with two sets of waymarks, it's easy to get confused.

165

BOLEA POPULATION 571

Bolea is built on two little hills and is another town built on the Moorish border. The highlight is Collegiate Church built in the 1530s and now a national monument which has a particularly fine Renaissance altarpiece. If 11km is too short a day, consider a walk up to the **Ermita de San Cristóbal**. It's well worth the effort. The chapel, which can only be accessed by foot, is built into a crevice in the cliffs above Bolea. To get to it follow a local footpath, the PR111, which joins the GR1 about a kilometre before it reaches Bolea from Loarre. From Bolea it's a 9km round-trip.

The town has accommodation at the Albergue A Gargalé (also a bar) (625 556 688) and rooms at Casa do Majo (see **www.turispain.com**) and Casa Rufino (974 272 505; **www.booking.com**).

STAGE 3
Bolea to Arguis

Start	Town centre, Bolea (700m)
Distance	19.5km
Ascent/Descent	1050m/700m
Grade	5/4
Walking time	7hr 15min
Maximum altitude	1384m

A great day's walk, including an easy but long climb which is rewarded with wonderful views of the Pico Gratal (1587m), the Pyrenees and Hoya de Huesca. There is nowhere to stop for lunch so take some food with you.

Follow the main road (Ctra Puibolea) to the northern edge of town (where the route entered the town on the previous stage). There, turn right and continue on the main road and head east (the GR1 and El Camino follow the same route). After 100 metres turn left onto a dirt road and head northeast. Continue northeast along the dirt road for 2.8km ignoring turns to the right and left (passing a reservoir after 2km), to where the route joins a path and heads into a valley alongside a stream.

Head northeast towards the mountains and ignore turns to the right and left. After 2km the route reaches a small reservoir.

Continue northeast and then east, past some houses. Start to climb turning north, after 800 metres, into a valley alongside a stream.

> To the right stands **Pico Gratal** a huge pyramid-shaped rock, a landmark visible from huge distances across the Hoya de Huesca. On a small rise to the side of the valley sits a very pretty chapel, the **Ermita de la Trinidad**.

Leaving the stream follow waymarks up a path into pine trees on the left-hand side of the valley and climb west then east around the head of the valley. If the weather is good the views across the plain to Bolea and the Hoya de Huesca will be excellent.

Bolea and the Hoya de Huesca

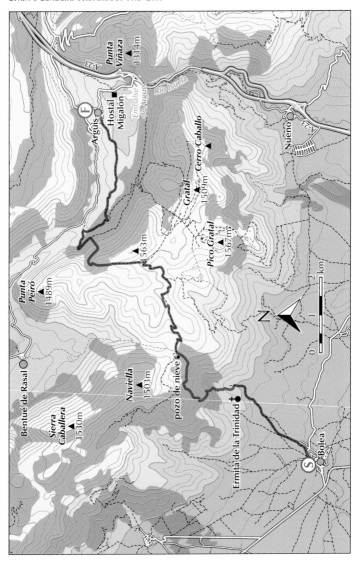

Follow the path up to the pass (featuring an old ice-making feature – a *pozo de nieve*). There the GR1 and El Camino split with El Camino taking a more direct and scenic route to Arguis. The GR1 continues north down the valley to the village of **Bentué de Rasal** before starting on a long road walk to Arguis.

El Camino turns east at the pass and climbs along a dirt trail across open moorland for 3.5km (getting ever closer to the **Pico Gratal**) before turning north and following a dirt road up along and across a valley. It leaves the dirt road at a low pass, with great views of the Pyrenees, about 1km later before heading down through a lovely beech forest. The route climbs to nearly 1400m before starting its descent.

Continue north reaching a junction after 600 metres (where there is the option of carrying onto the **Punte Peiró** further along the ridge) and turn east. Descend steeply along a path (with railings) through trees for 600 metres down the mountain to a dirt road and turn left (an option is presented here but ignore it). After 800 metres turn right at a junction (with great views north up the valley to the Sierra de Javierre). Head south along the valley

Pass before the descent

bottom for 700 metres and then east, through a heavily-eroded lunar landscape, into **Arguis**.

Arguis sits at the bottom of the valley next to a reservoir and is surrounded by the Sierra de Gratal. The motorway – the E7 – runs north–south along its eastern side. The Hostal Migalón, located to the southeast of the town (near a telecoms tower), provides great value and very pleasant accommodation (974 94 00 13). There is an off-road route to the hostal starting by the church but I've missed it twice and ended up on the road.

STAGE 4
Arguis to Nocito

Start	Hostal Migalón, Arguis (1040m)
Distance	19km
Ascent/Descent	1240m/1360m
Grade	5/5
Walking time	7hr 10min
Maximum altitude	1238m

Stage 4 is the first of two through the spectacular Parque Natural de la Sierra y Cañones de Guara. It's short, tough and the walking is wonderful. Depending on the time of year there are some not-to-be missed swimming or paddling opportunities.

The quickest way back to the route involves following a dirt trail on the opposite side of the road behind the small cement works. It runs parallel and beneath an elevated motorway. A short distance after crossing a stream, the waymarks reappear with the route climbing above the motorway as it disappears into the Monrepós tunnel. Follow the signs east up to the **Mesón Nuevo**.

Belsué

United the GR1 and El Camino head northeast for 3.5km down a valley and along a path through gorse to the semi-abandoned village of **Belsué**. ▶

From Belsué continue east for 500 metres through a gully (with amazing views back to the village) to a well-constructed but abandoned house. Just beyond the house the path meets a stream heading down a valley from the north. It's a beautiful stream with a smooth rock bottom the colour of polished York sandstone and a great place for a swim or a paddle.

Follow the south side of the stream (the **Río Fulmen**) and after 200 metres cross a footbridge. The valley then opens up.

On the hill immediately ahead is the ruined church of **Santa María de Belsué** and, to the south, the north end of a reservoir bearing the same name.

Stick to the northern side of the valley and continue on into the ruins of **Lúsera**, the first of many abandoned

The lovely Romanesque church here is dedicated to St Martin.

The second-best place on the GR1 for a swim

171

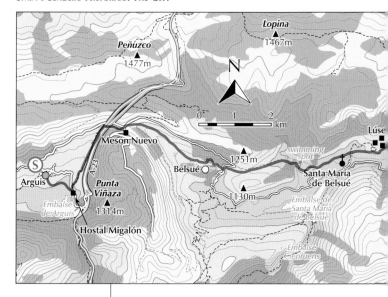

villages. Some of the ruins are in a precarious state and the route may be diverted.

From Lúsera, continue east, descend gently down to a stream and then climb steadily up a valley and over a low pass into another valley. After a tough climb

The precarious ruins at Lúsera

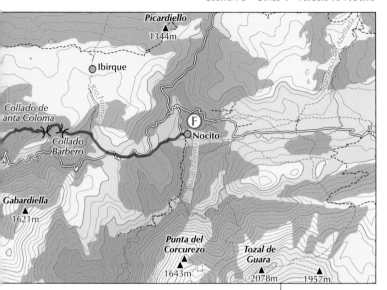

through trees, the route crosses the **Collado de Santa Coloma** and, shortly afterwards, a second pass, the **Collado Barbero**.

Ahead is **Tozal de Guara** (2078m) the highest peak in the Natural Park. If you are walking in March or early April it will be snow-covered.

From the pass follow the path downhill for 4km all the way to **Nocito**.

This tiny village, centred on a lovely bridge, sits nestled under Tozal de Guara. The campsite has a hostal and a restaurant (974 222 664; **www.camping vallenocito.com**), as does the Alberge la Mallata (which specialises in horse riding holidays) (974 340 149; **http://equitation.lamallata.com**). The hostal provides the best food.

STAGE 5
Nocito to Paúles de Sarsa

Start	Arched bridge, Nocito (918m)
Distance	36km
Ascent/Descent	1180m/1260m
Grade	5/4
Walking time	12hr
Maximum altitude	1211m
Note	You could split this stage into two by stopping at Rodellar, a climbing and canyoning centre, instead. To do this, take the GR1 to Bara and then follow signs to Rodellar, where there is accommodation; next day take a footpath from Rodellar to Paúles de Sarsa. Each leg is about 25km.

Stage 5 is long, tough but very beautiful. It visits a series of lonely abandoned villages with Nazare in particular enjoying a stunning location. If you have time (unlikely) there is a perfect spot for a swim. If the casa rural at Paúles de Sarsa is given advance notice a lift can be organised and a 2hr walk down a 7km road avoided.

From the bridge walk to the end of the row of houses, turn left and head northeast across a field into low trees. After emerging onto a road 600 metres later, cross it and follow a trail into more trees, turning east and heading to the **Santuario de San Urbez** (a 12th-century Romanesque building with 16th-century Renaissance additions).

Tozal de Guara immediately to the south dominates the views.

Continue east along a path through trees to the abandoned village of **Bentué de Nocito** and then on, still eastwards, through more open countryside to the next abandoned village, **Used**. ◄

After a gentle climb up the valley re-enter woodland and start a descent alongside a stream. After 4km turn south and follow the stream (now the **Río Used**) as it flows through a series of waterfall-filled pools. ◄ From

The pools, the 'Salto de Cardito', are the best places to swim on the whole of the GR1.

the streams walk southeast to a road and follow it east into **Bara**.

The best place on the GR1 for a swim

Head east from Bara and cross the stream south of the village (the bridge long gone). The waymarking on the other side is confusing but the route runs south for 200 metres and then climbs southeast along a path up a ridge. After a kilometre and a tough 300m of climb, it joins a dirt road and follows it for another kilometre into the abandoned village of **Nazare** complete with a pretty Romanesque church and wonderful views of the Pyrenees.

From Nazare head east along an old path lined with dry-stone walls across an open moor. After 2km the route reaches an old abandoned farmstead, the **Pardina Villanúa**. ▸

Continue east from the farmstead to the abandoned village of **Otin** (another kilometre).

Look inside: the paintwork is still intact.

Some of the houses at **Otin** are substantial and well finished with metal balconies. A sign points to the bar but it's a while since it served any drinks.

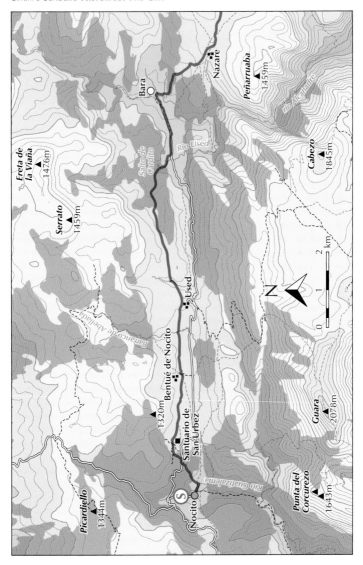

Head north from Otin along an old road, overgrown in places. After 1.2km the signs offer a detour down into the Oscuros de Otin canyon down to the **Río Mascún**. Continue north, where the waymarking is a little confusing, and after a kilometre turn right past the abandoned village of **Letusa**.

Leaving Letusa, continue east and make the long climb to yet another abandoned village – **Bagüeste**, a beautiful village centred on the dramatically located Romanesque Ermita de Santa Marina.

> Here the **waymarks** are confusing and the village itself is a mass of dangerous collapsing buildings and brambles. The safest option is to visit the village, come out again and then take a wide detour to the east (the terraces on the side of the village are very steep and also overgrown).

Pass the village well to the east along a trail and rejoin the route and turn north.

The Pyrenees from Otin

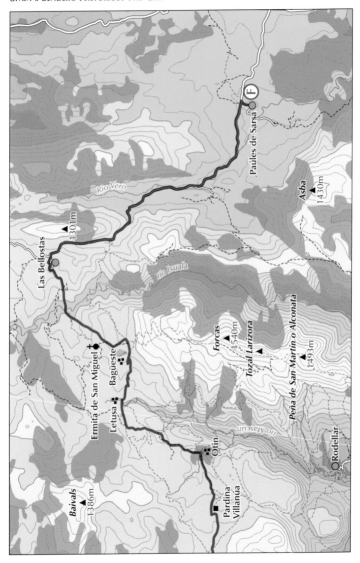

300 metres after turning north, and just before the **Ermita de San Miguel**, leave the dirt road, join a path on the right and head northeast. The turning is easily missed but the once on the path the new waymarkings are excellent. After 1.6km and a descent of 200m reach the bottom of the valley and cross a stream (Barranco de Balcez). Head east along the valley and down to another, larger stream, cross it and follow the path up the side of a valley to a dirt road and into the village of Las Bellostas.

> **Las Bellostas** is a pretty village where little sheep farms are occupied. Las Bellostas has a nearby road and the lift from Paúles de Sarsa can be picked up here.

The GR1 turns south onto the road and stays on it for nearly 7km. It's one of the longest stretches of road walking on the entire trip, which is amazing given how empty the countryside is and a lift to **Paúles de Sarsa** makes a lot of sense. As the route drops down the valley into a wide agricultural landscape, via a couple of ancient bridges and old mills, you return, once again, to the land of the living.

> Paúles de Sarsa is a tiny village but there are two places to stay: the Hostal El Cónder (974 343 095; **www.elcondor.es**); or the Casa Rural de Fina (974 343 132). The casa rural provides half board and a lift (for a very reasonable fee). There is also accommodation at the Sarsa de Surta at the Casa La Joya (974 343 148) – which is about 5km down the road from Las Bellostas.

STAGE 6

*Paúles de Sarsa to
Ligüerre de Cinca*

Start	Casa Rural, Paúles de Sarsa (866m)
Distance	24.5km
Ascent/Descent	480m/880m
Grade	4/4
Walking time	7hr 40min
Maximum altitude	962m

Stage 6 is easy but perhaps the least interesting day in this section. To improve it consider visiting the castle and church above Samitier and walking south along the ridge. The views from the top are spectacular. There are no lunch stops on the way.

Head north out of the village, back to the junction with the main road, turn right and head east for 100 metres. Following a sign, leave the road, and head northeast across a field towards a low ridge. After 400 metres climb onto the ridge, turn north and head to the edge of the village of **El Coscollar**.

Without going into the village turn east, cross a road and head along an old trail. After 100 metres leave the trail, continue east across a field and join another wall-lined path. Follow this path east for 2km, turning north along another old trail (which might be overgrown) just before reaching the main road into **Arcusa**.

> **Arcusa** is a small village with a large Renaissance church dedicated to San Estaban. Just to the north of the village are the remains of a tower, another part of the defensive line along the Moorish border. Hostel-style accommodation is available (**www. alberguedearcusa.com**).

Follow the main road north out of the village and, just before the old communal laundry, leave it and continue north along an old trail. After 250 metres turn east, climb along a path through trees and 600 metres later, at the top of the hill, join a dirt road. Continue east along the dirt road for 2.4km ignoring turn-offs to the south and north. The dirt road then turns west and crosses a small valley before turning east again. Continue along the dirt road through trees and downhill heading southeast until it emerges at a river below the village of **Castejón de Sobrarbe**. Cross the river, climb the steep bank and pass through the village. ▶

The large rotting church (Iglesia de la Asunción) is late Gothic and the remains of the castle can be seen on the mound above the village.

Leave the village on a path heading east and join a road after 100 metres. Continue along the road for 900 metres (cutting off a bend at one point), join an old trail, cross an open field and head into the hamlet of **La Pardina**. From La Pardina follow the road southeast for 2km leaving it as it turns and continue on a dirt road southeast. Ahead on the hillside is the village of **Samitier**.

SAMITIER

The castle at Samitier

Samitier is a small village, almost abandoned and situated on the slopes of a ridge bearing the same name. Dominating the village is a huge Romanesque tower, the only remaining feature of the original church. Its replacement, a more modest affair, is nearby.

Rooms are available in Samitier at the Casa La Abadía (620 203 948; www.casaabadia.com) although the website specifies a minimum stay of two nights.

The GR1 leaves the village to the south and follows a lovely path running parallel with a road below. After 1.5km a junction with a local path is reached providing the option of a shortcut to Ligüerre de Cinca. The GR1

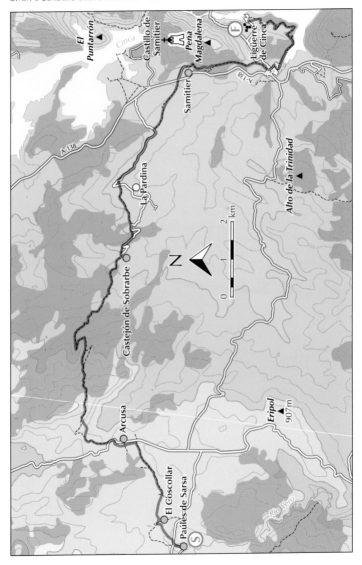

continues south, crosses a road, passes through a camp-
site and turns east along the shore of the Embalse de El
Grado I, past the ruins of a church (the Ermita de Santiàgo
Santa Bárbara) and then north to **Ligüerre de Cinca**.

> The abandoned village of Ligüerre de Cinca was taken
> over by the UGT (a trade union) and has been care-
> fully restored, to function as a holiday centre providing
> a wide range of accommodation including an excel-
> lent, good-value hotel (974 50 08 00; **www.liguerr
> edecinca.com** and **www.booking.com**).

High-level alternative finish
Instead of following the GR1 at Samitier, consider taking the dirt road northeast out of the village and climbing to the top of the ridge above. At the top is the
lovely Romanesque hermitage of San Emeterio and San
Celedonio, the **Castillo de Samitier** (both a church and
a castle), and a separate watchtower. The views from

Ligüerre de Cinca

183

the top are stunning, particularly to the north across the **Embalse di Mediano** to the Pyrenees. The buildings, constructed in the middle of the 11th century, made use of earlier defensive buildings built by the Moors, who were in residence until at least 1011.

Once on the top of the ridge there is a local footpath that heads south, eventually descending to another footpath with signs marking the way directly to **Ligüerre de Cinca**.

STAGE 7
Ligüerre de Cinca to Tierrantona

Start	Holiday centre, Ligüerre de Cinca (489m)
Distance	16.5km
Ascent/Descent	950m/770m
Grade	4/4
Walking time	6hr 30min
Maximum altitude	800m

This is a short but lovely stage featuring a spectacular walk through a gorge and along the side of the Embalse de Grado I. If there is time, walk up to Muro de Roda to enjoy yet more great views of the Pyrenees.

Leave the access road immediately to the west of the hotel facilities and follow a path as it runs north just above the side of the reservoir for a kilometre to a road. Follow the road east, cross the bridge and after 40 metres turn left onto a path into the gorge (**L'Entremon**) on the **Río Cinca**. The path, which at times has been carved out of the cliff face, is spectacular. Look out for San Emeterio, last seen at Samitier but now towering above the gorge.

Continue north for 2.5km and then climb out of the gorge along a path, through tunnels, to the right of a dam. From the top of the dam there are views of the Pyrenees in the distance and, more immediately, the top of the

L'Entremon

submerged **church** of the village of Mediano can be seen poking out above the waters of the reservoir.

Follow the shore of the reservoir to head north for 600 metres and then climb north and then east high above a valley. After 2km of hard walking the route descends, crosses a stream and makes a short climb into the small village **El Humo de Muro**.

> The main feature of the village is **Las Bodegas de Claveria**, a restored fortified house, which as well as a mini zoo featuring ostriches, has an excellent restaurant and accommodation (974 341 044; www.lasbodegasdeclaveria.es).

From El Humo de Muro take the road north, leave it after 200 metres (the road is now heading west) and follow a path that climbs steeply through trees. After 800 metres cross a dirt road and continue north for 1.8km, to a ruined farmstead. Join a dirt road and at a junction 700 metres later turn right.

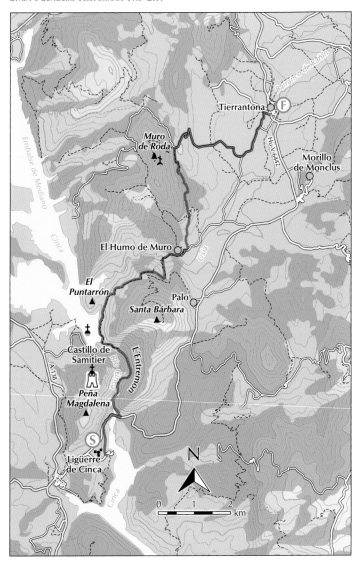

Detour to Muro de Roda

For an excursion, turn left and head up the hill for about a kilometre to visit the ruins at **Muro de Roda** and the wonderful fortified Romanesque church of Santa Maria. The views north to the Pyrenees from this spot are fantastic.

Continue along the dirt road zig-zagging down the hill. Once the trail has levelled out follow it east and then north for 3km to **Tierrantona**, a village right at the heart of the Fueva basin.

> The church is Romanesque and dedicated to the Assumption. Rooms can be found in the Casa Escartin (974 50 70 21) and the Casa Puyuelo (974 507 028; www.casapuyuelo.com and www.booking.com).

STAGE 8
Tierrantona to Salinas de Trillo

Start	Casa Puyuelo, Tierrantona (635m)
Distance	16km
Ascent/Descent	690m/560m
Grade	2/4
Walking time	5hr 30min
Maximum altitude	1033m

Poor waymarking and some overgrown trails make this a challenging stage. Fortunately it's not too long and the accommodation at the end is delightful.

From the bar head southeast along the main road to the edge of the village. Just before reaching a bridge over a wide gravelly stream turn right and head south on a dirt track on the western side of a river for 2km. Cross the river here (very shallow for most of the year) and turn east. After 900 metres cross the road running north–south and continue east for 300 metres, then head south and

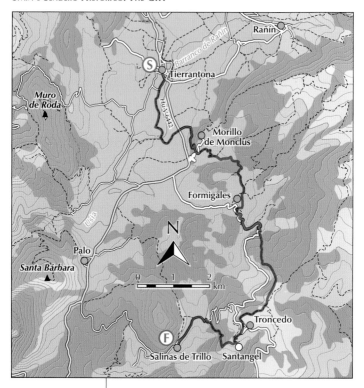

join a road 800 metres later. Turn left and follow the road east for about 100 metres before leaving it and continuing east along a dirt trail. The route skirts the tiny village of **Morillo de Monclus** with its Romanesque church dedicated to St Christopher.

The route to Formigales is poorly waymarked. Follow the dirt road east then south for 800 metres before turning east at a junction with another dirt road. After 300 metres leave the dirt road and follow a path east for 800 metres through trees along a valley and down to a stream. Cross the stream and climb gently out of the valley emerging from the trees onto a dirt road and into open arable countryside. After 800 metres the dirt road arrives at a junction and the route continues south although the ancient path is now an overgrown trench and impassable. Walk through the field alongside the original path reaching the village fountain after 200 metres. Unless the route has been cleared it will be necessary to turn right, head across the field and follow the road into the village of **Formigales**.

> **Formigales** has a fine fortified house (Palacio de los Mur), currently in the process of being restored, and a 16th-century church dedicated to Santa Eulàlia.

Pass through the village and rejoin the road to the south. Leave the main road and follow an old road running parallel to it east to a bridge over a small stream. Rejoin the main road and follow it south for about 200 metres to a GR1 sign. Follow the dirt road up the hill (initially the dirt road zig-zags but then straightens out) south for 200 metres to a cairn. Turn left at the cairn and follow

Recycled fencing

The turn-off from the dirt road is easily missed.

a forest path heading east and then turning south. ◄ Continue south along the forest path, climbing all the time, for 700 metres to a pass and open views. Here the path turns into a trail and it's a pleasant 2km walk into **Troncedo**.

> **Troncedo** is a tiny but very lovely hilltop village. Originally there were probably two hamlets, one built around the castle and parish church (a Romanesque church dedicated to St Michael) at the southern end of the village and the other, with a church dedicated to St Stephen, at the northern end. The Castle of Troncedo, with its splendid tower, was probably built in the middle of the 11th century as part of the defence line of castles designed to keep out recently displaced Moors.

> Pass the castle on its western side and head down towards the hamlet at **Santangel**. On the sharp bend before the hamlet is a post (no markings and easily missed) and earth steps leading down to a path (initially overgrown). Join what turns into a lovely path, follow it for 1.8km west and down into a valley to a road. Follow the road into **Salinas de Trillo**.

SALINAS DE TRILLO POPULATION <20

Salinas de Trillo gets its name from the saline springs that emerge in the gorge below the village. It has a particularly attractive Romanesque church dedicated to the Assumption and a large fortified house, the Casa Palacio, built in the 16th century.

Accommodation is provided at the Casa Bielsa (974 34 10 69) which seeks to feed guests entirely on home produce – this includes the wine, a litre of which is provided with breakfast next morning.

STAGE 9

Salinas de Trillo to Graus

Start	Village centre, Salinas de Trillo (777m)
Distance	26km
Ascent/Descent	900m/1210m
Grade	4/4
Walking time	9hr
Maximum altitude	1149m

The final stage is long but easy. It's a walk of two halves: the first mainly along a forest path and the second across open moorland with excellent views, along an old but never-ending transhumance route. There is nowhere to stop but it's worth trying the hostel in Pano.

From Salinas de Trillo follow the road southwest and head down the valley. Take the left fork in the road after 800 metres and continue down to **Trillo** and its large but increasingly derelict and abandoned church. Leave the road and head down and around into the valley immediately to the north of the church; the route may be hard to follow at this point and overgrown. Head down to the stream and follow it southwest for a few metres, then turn left and follow a path up along a stream for 200 metres to a dirt trail.

Turn right onto the trail and follow it south, up the hill through trees, for 800 metres to the hamlet of **Caneto**. Pass through Caneto and head southeast for 300 metres, where the route leaves the dirt road, and continue southeast and then south. Follow the trail through trees heading southeast for 2.7km to a dirt road.

Follow the dirt road southwest (along a gentle ridge), turning sharply southeast after 200 metres and head south across a wooded valley. On the south side of the valley the route leaves the dirt road and follows a trail southwest then southeast, emerging at the little settlement of **Pano**.

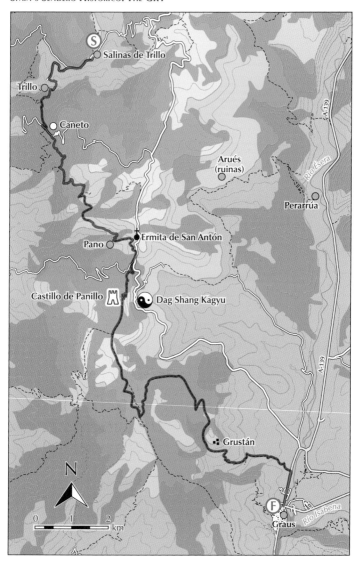

Starting the long trail to Graus

Pano is a tiny village straddling a ridge. After being abandoned by the locals it is now being lovingly restored on an ecological basis by the Pano Foundation, a trust led by Swiss entrepreneur Kurt Fridez. On my last visit the function of the place was a little unclear but the host was very welcoming and provided a free lunch!

From Pano head east along the road past the Romanesque **Ermita de San Antón** for 1.1km, to a junction near a small church (Ermita de la Virgen de la Collada) and take a dirt road south running parallel with the road below it. The route zig-zags its way gently to the top of a ridge and the **Castillo de Panillo**, a tiny Romanesque castle built on Moorish foundations and key to the defence of the Fueva valley.

Continue south along an open ridge for 3.5km.

The **Pyrenees** to the north and the huge reservoirs to the west and south provide excellent views. To the east, and at the bottom of the valley, watch out for the **Dag Shang Kagyu** – a Buddhist temple providing a welcome touch of Nepal to northern Spain.

After 3.5km the route arrives at a junction. Turn sharp left and follow the dirt road initially northeast. After 5km you pass through the abandoned village of **Grustán** centred on a stunning Romanesque church dedicated to Santa María de Grustán. Continue east downhill, ignoring turns to the left and right, until after 3km the route reaches a busy road. Head south along the side of the road into **Graus**.

GRAUS POPULATION 3429

Graus

After days of tiny, often abandoned villages, Graus will feel like a metropolis. It has some fine buildings and an old medieval core, the Barrichós. It was a significant town for both the Moors and the medieval rulers of Aragón. Perhaps the most important building, sitting high up on the cliffs to the western side of the town, is the Basilica of the Virgen of La Peña. The original Romanesque church was radically extended in the 16th century – including the construction of cloisters which provide amazing views across the town and valley – and the majority of the building dates back to that time. It was burnt down in 1936 at the beginning of the Civil War but restored in the 1940s.

Graus is an important location in the history of the conflict with the Moors and was the site of a battle in 1063 where a young El Cid had his first taste of warfare.

There is a lot of accommodation in Graus but the Lleida is particularly good value and the bar seems to be the centre of town life (974 540 925; **www.hotel-lleida. com** and **www.booking.com**). Alternatives include the Casa Roque (974 54 08 65) and the Bodegas de Arnés (974 540 300; **www.bodegasdearnes.com**).

6 GRAUS TO GIRONELLA

Looking back to the Castell de Girbeta

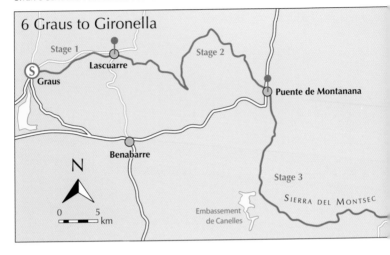

6 Graus to Gironella

Stage 1

Lascuarre

Stage 2

S Graus

Puente de Montanana

Benabarre

N

0   5 km

Stage 3

SIERRA DEL MONTSEC

Embassement
de Canelles

This section continues the journey east through the Pre-Pyrenees and visits some of the GR1's most memorable scenery.

The most dramatic feature is the Sierra del Montsec crossed during Stages 3 to 6. Here an east–west slab of cretaceous rock has been sliced

The ruined church at Rùbies

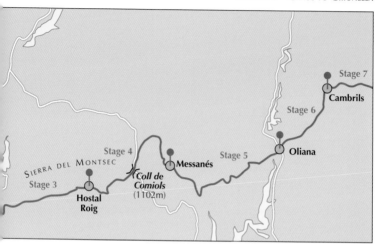

in three by two rivers draining down from the Pyrenees. Deep gorges split the range into three and the GR1 goes through the best of them. Each slab of mountain is a 'montsec' in its own right (Rùbies, D'Ares and d'Estall).

Vegetation-wise the scenery is subtly different from the previous section. It's drier than anything experienced so far and more obviously Mediterranean. Scrub is everywhere with rosemary, thyme, broom and rock rose dominating the vegetation, and the landscape feels harsher and slightly more barren.

Abandoned villages and farmsteads continue to feature but the settlements are smaller, a consequence perhaps of poorer land and a lower historic population. Some of the settlements feature more Marche

Hispánica castle ruins. The mountains formed an important defensive line for both Moors and Christians (Balaguer was the most northerly Moorish city up until the 10th century).

ACCESS AND ACCOMMODATION

Although neither Graus at the beginning or Gironella at the end of Section 6 are connected to the national rail network the bus services from both are excellent. For Graus and connections to Zaragoza go to http://alosa. avanzabus.com. Gironella is not a particularly interesting place but it is accessible and it should be possible to catch one of the frequent buses at the end of the short final stage and make the 90-minute journey to Barcelona down the Autopista de Monteserrat

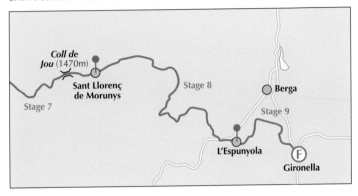

to fly home on the same day. The times for the buses from Gironella to Barcelona can be found at www.alsa. es.

Sparsely populated country-side, even by GR1 standards, means fewer places to stay, and finding nightly accommodation on the route itself is sometimes impossible. Only the superhiker will attempt to walk through to the next place and a couple of taxi journeys are usually required to make the itinerary feasible.

Although not a difficult walk there are, even without accommodation difficulties, a couple of days that are challenging by GR1 standards. The waymarking, however, continues to be excellent, particularly once the route enters Catalonia.

SECTION 6: KEY INFORMATION	
Distance	263.5km
Total ascent	9680m
Total descent	9670m
Alternative schedule	Consider staying for an extra day in Ager and exploring the Montsec d'Ares – the hostel there is a specialist outdoor centre and the manager will happily provide advice on the best things to do.

STAGE 1

Graus to Lascuarre

Start	Town centre, Graus (456m)
Distance	21.5km
Ascent/Descent	520m/580m
Grade	3/3
Walking time	6hr 30min
Maximum altitude	680m

Stage 1 is a pleasant and easy walk through a predominantly agricultural landscape. Much of the route runs parallel with the Río Isábena. There is a restaurant at Capella which, if open, could be used for a mid-morning stop.

From the town centre near the bridge, follow the river path south rejoining the main road after 600 metres. After 200 metres turn left and go east across the bridge.

El Monasterio de la Virgen de la Peña

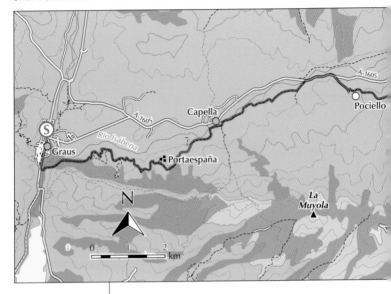

The **Puente de Abajo** on the Río Ésera is the first in an impressive series of ancient bridges crossed on the GR1's journey through Catalonia. Originally Roman, it was rebuilt in the 12th century and offers a fantastic view back to the monastery El Monasterio de la Virgen de la Peña.

Continue east for 4km through undulating wooded countryside along the southern bank of the **Río Isábena** to the abandoned village of **Portaespaña**.

Portaespaña, with its Romanesque church dedicated to St Margaret, is almost overgrown but the views north towards the Pyrenees are excellent.

Follow a dirt road southeast out of the village and down through a field before turning east then northeast across a scrubby landscape. Head towards the river, join a dirt road and follow it to **Capella**.

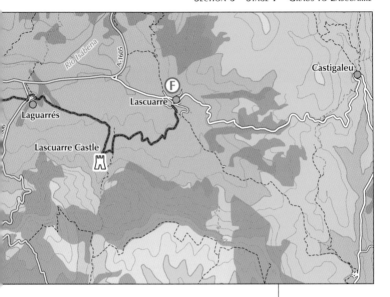

At **Capella**, which is dominated by a huge grain tower, there is another striking seven-arch Romanesque bridge. The village has a restaurant that might be able to make you a *café con leche*.

From the bridge continue east for 3km along a dirt trail running parallel with the river until it reaches a road. Follow the road east, turn right after 800 metres and head into the hamlet of **Pociello**.

From Pociello follow a dirt road heading east out of the village. The route carries on up a hill and then east for 2km to the village of **Laguarrés**.

Laguarrés also has a large 16th-century Renaissance church (Iglesia de la Asunción) and a smaller, prettier Romanesque chapel just to its north.

Follow a dirt road east then southeast and head across fields for 2.4km before turning south. After 800 metres turn east and continue for 400 metres over a slight ridge. Just to the south of the trail is Lascuarre Castle. After 400 metres turn north and continue for 3km to **Lascuarre** itself.

LASCUARRE POPULATION 136

Lascuarre was an important border town for both Moorish and early Christian rulers of Aragón, and evidence of their attempts to defend it is everywhere. There is a debate about the Tower of the Moors with some saying it was built by the Moors, others saying it was built by Christians, and others that it was a fortified house built in the 17th century.

The castle was definitely originally Moorish. It was captured by Sancho III as part of his reconquest, refortified, and became the most important of four castles built to secure the area. The village itself has a defensive format and remnants of the old walls are still present. The historic significance of the town is evident from the number of religious buildings. The huge main church is 16th-century Gothic/Renaissance and sits alongside the ruins of an abbey. Outside the village are the Romanesque chapel of St Martin, the remains of a Trinitarian convent and the ruins of another church.

Accommodation is available at the Antigua Casa Catones (974 544 256; **www.booking.com**) although it's not always open so it's best to check ahead.

STAGE 2

Lascuarre to Puente de Montañana

Start	Village square, Lascuarre (643m)
Distance	33km; shortcut: 26.3km
Ascent/Descent	1140m/1160m
Grade	3/2
Walking time	11hr; shortcut: 9hr
Maximum altitude	1050m

Stage 2 is a long and interesting walk but has no obvious places to stop for refreshments. To make it more manageable consider taking a shortcut by missing out the walk to Luzás.

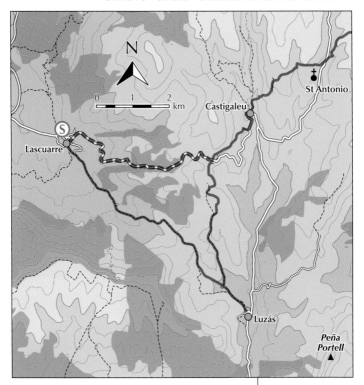

Shortcut avoiding Luzás

Take the main road east out of Lascuarre for 5.5km, until the GR1 sign points north, 800 metres past the junction with the dirt track coming up from Luzás on the right.

From the square head southwest along the Calle la Monja, the way into the village, and head down to a small bridge. After crossing the bridge pass the junction with yesterday's route and continue southeast along a dirt road. Continue southeast and then south for 5km ignoring turns to left and right (crossing a cañada real after 4km). The original path leaves the dirt road after 5km but

Luzás castle with its polygonal 11th-century tower

it's overgrown so stay with the dirt road and continue south then southeast into **Luzás**.

> **Luzás** is small village on the banks of the Río Tolva. The most spectacular feature is remains of Luzás castle with its polygonal 11th-century tower. The village also has a 13th-century Romanesque church dedicated to St Christopher.

Head back out of the village on the same route used to enter it and turn north after a kilometre. Continue along a dirt track for 3.8km to the main road from Lascuarre (again the original route has become overgrown). ◄

The shortcut rejoins here.

Turn east and follow the road for 800 metres where GR1 signs points north. The waymarks at this point are hard to follow. Continue northeast along the side of a valley. After 1.2km the route hits a dirt road, turns east down into the valley past a cemetery and joins the main road following it north into **Castigaleu**.

Castigaleu is a small village at the bottom of a valley and dominated by an austere Gothic church dedicated to St Martin. A pretty Romanesque chapel dedicated to San Isidro sits on the hill west of town.

Follow the main road through the village, turn left onto a dirt trail and head north along a valley on the west side of a stream. After 400 metres turn east, cross the stream and climb up the side of the valley. The waymarking here is again difficult to follow. After climbing part way up the ridge the route turns north and heads along a dirt trail towards a farmstead before turning east again along a path and completing the ascent of the ridge. It descends into the next shallow valley and climbs out of it, heading east across a field to trees. It then descends through trees, passes the tiny **chapel** of St Antonio and heads down to a road. It's 3km from Castigaleu to the road.

Cross the road and follow a path north down to a stream. Cross the stream and climb up the side of the valley along an ancient overgrown trail that heads first north and then swings east. After a kilometre it reaches the small abandoned village of **Monesma de Benabarre** with its huge church.

Turn south at the village and follow a path along the western flank of the Tozal del Puyol (1236m).

If you can muster the energy to climb to the top you will find the ruins of the **Castillo de Monesma** and, on a clear day, enjoy some great views north to the Pyrenees.

The walk along the sandy flank of the mountain is tough and the path is eroded, hard to follow and overgrown in places. After a kilometre it reaches the largely abandoned village of **Sarroca de Monesma**.

Leave the village along a path on its western side and head south then east down to a dirt road. Follow the dirt road down to a crossroads and head south-southwest. After 400 metres take a left-hand fork and head east.

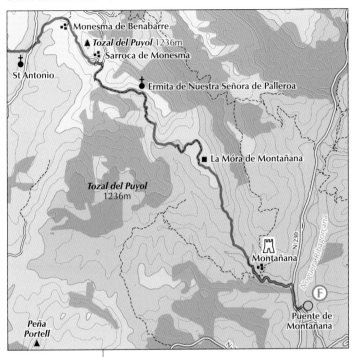

Follow this trail east then south down a valley for 3km. After 1.5km, just before the trail turns south, pass the little Ermita de Nuestra Señora de Palleroa.

After 3km turn east, follow a path for 600 metres and join a dirt road. Follow the dirt road for 1.6km to the farmstead **La Móra de Montañana**. From here follow an ancient paved path, walled in places, for 3km southeast along an increasingly obvious ridge. At the end of the ridge is the historic village of **Montañana**.

Although now largely abandoned **Montañana**'s unique defensive position has left a legacy of impressive buildings. The GR1 enters the village from above on an ancient paved pathway and descends down to

Approaching Montañana

the huge Romanesque church of St Mary, sitting dramatically at the end of the promontory which divides two gorges. It has a large tower and the arch over the main door is finely carved.

After another short descent the route reaches a huge defensive tower with a bridge over a natural moat. From here look across the narrow valley to a pretty Romanesque chapel dedicated to San Juan. From the tower you enter into the tightly packed village of centuries-old stone buildings over a single-arched Gothic footbridge.

From Montañana follow the main road east for a kilometre to meet the busy N-230. Follow this south for 500 metres to the town of **Puente de Montañana**.

PUENTE DE MONTAÑANA POPULATION 119

Puente de Montañana is a small town on the boundary between Aragón and Catalonia. The town centre is on the eastern bank of the Río Noguera-Ribagorçana which you cross via a Himalayan-style suspension footbridge (built in 1938 by the Zapadores de Tenerife – army engineers).

The village has two hostals, both near the main road on the river's western bank as you approach the suspension bridge. The Isidro is functional and good value (974 542 155; **www.hostalisidro.com**) but the Condes de Ribagorza (974 54 21 94) is an alternative.

STAGE 3
Puente de Montañana to Àger

Start	Hostal Isidro, Puente de Montañana (540m)
Distance	27km
Ascent/Descent	1040m/980m
Grade	5/4
Walking time	9hr 30min
Maximum altitude	720m

Today's walk through the Noguera-Ribagorçana gorge, part of the Congost de Mont-rebei Nature Reserve, is one of the highlights of the whole route, spoilt just slightly by a road walk on the approach. A GR1 variant, which is difficult to manage from an accommodation perspective, misses the gorge and is not described in the notes below.

Cross the footbridge into Puente de Montañana and head through the gate into the main square. Join the Calle Arrabal at the eastern side of the square and head southeast out of town to join a waymarked path. Pass under the main road bridge before joining a metalled road after 2km and following it for the next 3.5km. Although the walking itself is dull the views ahead to the opening of the gorge are dramatic.

The road eventually reaches a car park and a path that leads into the gorge.

Opposite to the west is the tiny 11th-century **Ermita de la Mare de Déu del Congost** and above, more dramatic and guarding the entrance to the gorge, is an old Moorish watchtower, the **Castell de Girbeta**.

Head southwest then follow the path south, scrambling over rock to enter the **gorge** on a pathway carved into its vertical eastern wall. At times the gorge is only 20 metres across and it's impossible to see the top of the

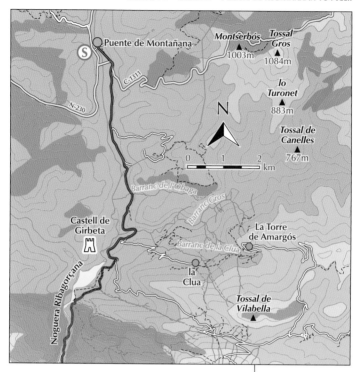

cliffs that tower above. The path is breathtaking but completely safe providing you are sensible.

Continue south to where the cliffs, fan-like, start to diverge.

> On the opposite side of the gorge is a spectacular, recently constructed, suspended **wooden path** that zigzags its way up the cliff face (providing access for climbers). The route to it is signposted from the GR1.

Take a gentler route and follow a path south through trees, climbing 280m over the next 2.5km. The views

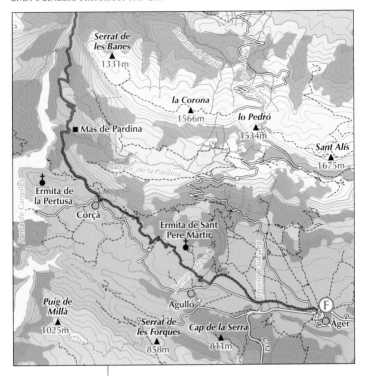

back to the gorge, with the **Castell de Girbeta** clearly visible at its other end, and south to the mountains surrounding the Embassement de Canelles reservoir, are excellent.

Continue south and go down into a valley, past a ruined farmhouse (the **Mas de Pardina**) and up the other side. ◄

From the promontory continue southeast along a narrow road for 2km down to the village of **Corça**. The village has a bar/restaurant – El Congost – and is the perfect place for a well-earned lunch stop.

Returning from lunch to the narrow road, GR1 signs point the way along a route that leaves the road

To the west of the trail, perfectly located on a promontory high above the reservoir, is the tiny Romanesque chapel the Ermita de la Pertusa.

In the Noguera-Ribagorçana gorge

and climbs northeast past a house then swings southeast. Initially a path, then a dirt road, it climbs gently up the valley side before starting a long descent. On the other side of the valley is the village of **Agulló**.

Continue southeast for 7km. The valley opens up and becomes increasingly arable, and Àger should be visible in the distance. At the junction with a dirt road running down to Agulló is the little stone **Ermita de Sant Pere Màrtir**.

The Ermita de la Pertusa

ÀGER POPULATION 594

Àger has a splendid location, climbing up a hill in the middle of the valley with great views north to the cliffs of the Montsec d'Ares. The defensive value of the location was recognised by the Romans and the Moors and shortly after the reconquest a substantial castle and church was built on top of the hill in Romanesque style. It's a good place to end a day's walk and the ancient unspoilt medieval core of the town is well worth exploring.

The Alberg Vall d'Àger (687 536 571; www.albergvalldager.com) in the main street just down from a bar provides food and hostel-style accommodation (some of it in dormitories), and will provide a lift next day if you want one. The nearest hotel-style accommodation is at the Cal Maciarol (615 512 701, www.calmaciarol.com) about 2km to the northwest of the town.

STAGE 4

Àger to Hostal Roig

Start	Village centre, Àger (642m)
Distance	31km; variant: 33km
Ascent/Descent	1640m/1160m
Grade	4/4
Walking time	11hr 20min; variant: 11hr
Maximum altitude	1590m

Stage 4 is a long day with one of the hardest climbs of the whole GR1. It is, however, very rewarding and, if you are lucky with the weather, you will enjoy great views of the Pyrenees and much wonderful walking. The least interesting part is from Àger to the bridge over the reservoir – the Embassament de Camarasa – the bridge beyond the railway station. The manager at the Alberg Vall d'Àger will provide a lift down the reservoir. If he takes you to road marker K46, this will take nearly 13km, or three hours, off the day.

Unfortunately the days when Hostal Roig provided accommodation are long gone and a taxi down to Vilanova de Meià has to be organised to reach any accommodation at the other end.

From the centre of Àger head north to the main road and turn east. Just past the bus stop turn left and head northeast past an open-air swimming pool. Leave the metalled road and continue north along a dirt road northeast for 2km, ignoring turns to the south after 800 metres and to the north 100 metres further on. Continue with the dirt road as it turns east ignoring the turn to the north after 400 metres and another after a further 600 metres. Follow the now-meandering track for 2.3km and take a right-hand fork at a junction. 200 metres later turn east and continue for 3.5km to the tiny village of **L'Ametlla de Montsec**.

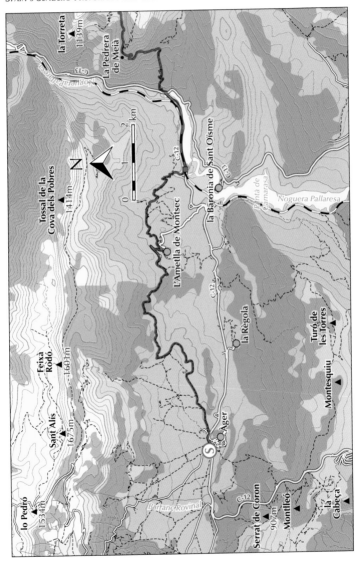

Follow the dirt road leaving the village from its north-eastern side. After 1.9km and two junctions, take a right turn onto a path and follow it down to another dirt road. Turn left and follow the dirt road for a kilometre as it swings east and south down the valley. The route then leaves the road and continues down the valley along a path to the railway station and road.

From the railway station the official route has recently changed and now crosses the road and follows the western bank of the reservoir for 2km east but it's easier to stay on the road and save energy for the big climb.

After crossing the bridge and the main road turn right past a bus stop and then left on a dirt track heading up the mountainside. Follow it up into trees for 700 metres and leave it to join a path taking a more direct line east. Stay on the path for some 800 metres (twice crossing the dirt road that's taking a gentler route), passing the ruins of a farmstead on the way. The route rejoins the dirt road before turning left after 100m and going north along a path. It then follows a spectacular rocky path before turning east and zig-zagging its way up to the ruins of an old quarry, **La Pedrera de Meià**.

> As you cross the scree, enjoy the amazing views north to the **Congost de Terradets** (a similar feature to the Noguera Ribagorçana walked through in the previous stage), and beyond that to the Pyrenees.

After the scree the route turns definitively east and for a time follows the old quarry road before joining a path and diving into a forest of box and evergreen oak. Following a valley up the side of a mountain the path briefly loses height, crosses a stream and then climbs again and at last reaches the abandoned hamlet of **Rùbies**.

> The setting of **Rùbies** is lovely, very remote and sheltered under huge cliffs. The ruined church is Romanesque. Everything is overgrown with brambles and clematis and you can almost hear the conversations of previous inhabitants.

Views north from the ridge above Rùbies

Variant exit on foot to Vilanova de Meià

If you would prefer to walk to your night's accommodation, rather than stick with the GR1 to Hostal Roig and get a taxi from there, follow the dirt road to the east of Rùbies down to the village of **Santa Maria de Meià** and on along a road into **Vilanova de Meià**. It should be a pleasant 12km walk, only 2km more than the walk to Hostal Roig.

Above Rùbies is a huge cliff with two distinct gashes. The one on the left is the **Portella Blanca**. The GR1 leaves Rùbies on its northern side and takes a faint path directly up the to the cliff face. The path is steep, difficult to follow and local goatherds have created a number of alternative routes. Persist and after the initial gullied scree the 'path', which seems to be heading for the wrong gash, becomes evident. After a tough climb up the cliff side through wonderful natural vegetation it heads into a little gap in the rock face and through it up onto a grassy mountain top.

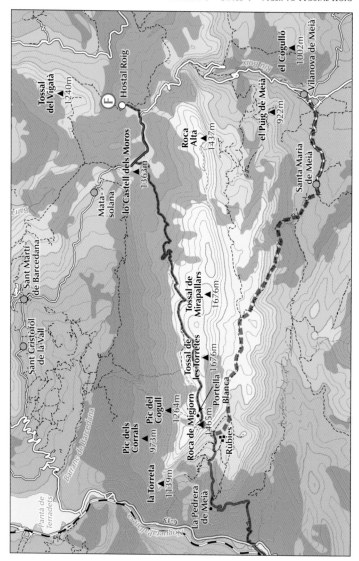

The **views** from the top are excellent in all directions, particularly north to the gorge and beyond that to the Pyrenees.

At the top the signs are a little confusing with green signs pointing down to Sant Salvador. This is an option (it returns to the GR1 later) but after climbing 1200m since leaving the road near the reservoir, most walkers will want to stay high. Head east, parallel with the cliff, and after a short climb join a dirt road and follow it east for 4km where the route leaves the road and joins a path which rejoins the road after a kilometre. Continue on the dirt road for 2.5km before joining a path down for the last 600 metres to **Hostal Roig** where you will be hoping that your taxi awaits.

Vilanova de Meià is 12km away to the south. The taxi driver (973 415 029) Antonia, also runs the town supermarket and provides accommodation. Dinner (and accommodation) can also be found at Casa Cirera (973 415 081; www.casacirera.com).

STAGE 5
Hostal Roig to Messanés

Start	Village centre, Hostal Roig (1097m)
Distance	25.5km
Ascent/Descent	600m/1080m
Grade	4/4
Walking time	8hr 20min
Maximum altitude	1215m

Stage 5 is easier but continues to follow the same ridge as it bends around to the north. Much of the walk is through trees but when the views open up they are excellent.

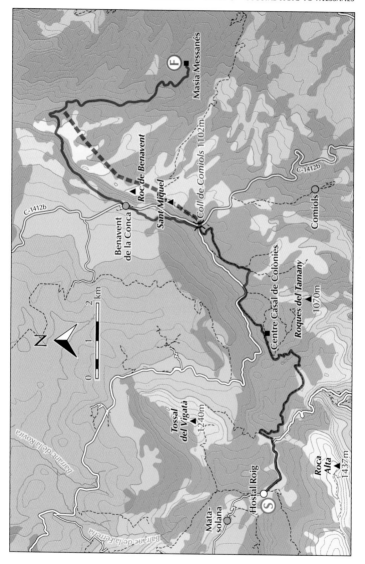

From the end of the valley there is a good view south to the ridge and a distinct part of the escarpment known as the Roca dels Ares.

Follow the road south then east for 1.8km (this is the same road taken by the taxi – to avoid the road walk get out earlier). Follow a dirt road north for 300 metres up a valley, turn right across a field and then join a path heading south through trees. ◄

Continue along the path as it heads back to the ridge, turn east and after 3.5km drop into a valley.

Cross the valley and climb out of it heading north and leaving the original trail. Continue for 800 metres and turn right onto a dirt road and head east. After 600 metres you reach the **Centre Casal de Colònies** 'Bon Repòs', a beautiful old farmstead that provides dormitory accommodation for educational groups.

Continue past the hostel (ignoring the right-hand turn) for 1.4km and, after turning southeast, join a road. Follow the road as it bends northeast for 300 metres and take a right-hand turn off the road onto a path. Follow the path east for 500 metres and then take a left turn onto a dirt road. Continue north along the dirt road for 900 metres, take a right-hand turn and head northeast. After 900 metres (passing under power lines on the way) turn left, past an old petrol station and down to the **Coll de Comiols** (1102m).

If a taxi were needed this would be a good place to arrange a **pick-up**. It's also out of the trees with views north across valley (the Conca Dellà) to the Pyrenees.

The GR1 now heads north and down into the valley.

High-level variant

The alternative approach, avoiding the descent and perhaps with better views, involves joining the local route, signposted on the other (right-hand) side of the main road, and following a path and dirt road northeast along the eastern flank of the ridge. After 8km the dirt road turns decisively to the southeast with the GR1 descending from the ridge at the same point.

To follow the GR1 cross the road immediately to the north of the abandoned petrol station and join a dirt road heading northeast and parallel with the main road. Follow a path (the old road – overgrown in places) for 2.3km down to the village of **Benavent de la Conca**, a tiny village with no services.

Benavent de la Conca and the Roc de Benavent

After joining the main road just before the village, follow it past the old part of the village, cross it and join a dirt road on the right-hand side. To the east are the cliffs of the **Roc de Benavent**. Follow a pleasant wooded trail for 2.3km leaving it as it turns left, and continue up a fairly gentle path to the top of the cliffs. ▶

Out of the trees the views across the valley from the top of the hill are excellent.

From the ridge the route descends down through a dry, scrubby and largely empty landscape. Turn left onto a dirt road just beyond the brow of a hill and follow it down into a valley past an abandoned farmstead. Take the right turn at a junction after 1.3km.

Continue south for 500 metres, past a left-hand turn and ignore another left-hand turn 1.5km later. After 800 metres the route turns left (ignoring a dirt road that continues south) and after another 700 metres passes a

221

farmstead and ignores a left-hand turn. Continue down-hill, ignoring minor turnings, for 3km to the little hotel at **Messanés** (there are signs to it from the top of the pass). On the opposite side of the valley from the hotel is the tiny village of Sant Cristòfol de la Donzell.

Restaurant Masia Massanés sits in splendid isolation on top of a little hill. It has rooms and provides excellent food (973 296 018; **www.masiamassanes.com**).

STAGE 6
Massanés to Oliana

Start	Restaurant Masia Massanés (630m)
Distance	26.5km
Ascent/Descent	690m/890m
Grade	3/3
Walking time	8hr 30min
Maximum altitude	990m

A long walk but easy and with no serious climbs. The first part involves a lovely forest path; the second a walk along a long dirt road but with great views; and the last part a walk across a flat valley bottom surrounded by towering cliffs. Peramola can be reached in time for a late lunch although be aware that the bar/restaurant there is not always open.

Leave the restaurant, return to the dirt road followed on the previous stage, and continue east down the valley for 2km. At the bottom of the valley leave the road and cross a bridge to the east side of the valley and follow a dirt road south. After 100 metres leave the dirt road (which swings east) and join an overgrown path that follows the track of an old road heading south above the stream.

Follow the path for 1.3km (passing a **fish farm** on the other side of the valley). Ignore a forest road heading east and continue through trees as the path climbs

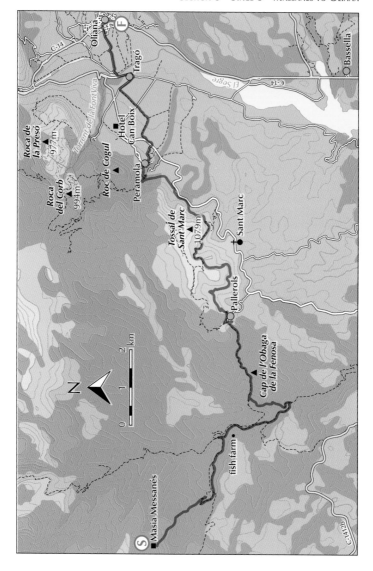

223

Approaching Pallerols and looking back to the Montsec de Rùbies

gently around the valley turning east and then (into another valley) north. The waymarks in the trees are hard to follow but after a short while a distinct path re-emerges. Continue north for 300 metres, descend down to a stream, cross it and head east. Continue east along a well-marked path through trees for 3km to **Pallerols**.

> **Pallerols** is a tiny but scenically located village high on a hillside. The church, Romanesque in parts, is dedicated to San Esteban.

The route after Pallerols is along a tedious dirt road around and then down the mountain. The views, however, are excellent.

◄ Follow the signs north from the village and after 200 metres turn right. After 2.7km, and generally heading east, pass an abandoned Romanesque church dedicated to **Sant Marc**. Continue along the same dirt road for another 2.5km, leaving it and joining a path as the road turns south at a sharp hairpin. Continue along the path (above and parallel to a conspicuously empty modern road) for 1.4km, underneath the cliffs of **Tossal de Sant Marc**, until it joins a dirt road. Follow the dirt road for a kilometre until you get to the main road into **Peramola**. The GR1 takes you into the town through a small park on a trail running parallel with the road.

Peremola is a charming town nestling underneath the mountains with a range of services. It's a good place to stop for lunch. There is luxury accommodation located to the east of the town (a walk of about 2km) at the **Hotel Can Boix** (973 470 266; **www.canboix.com**), or, if a cheaper option is required, you could stay at La Masia Forné (973 470 461) located in town.

Leave the town along the main road heading east, turn left at an even bigger road and follow it for 100 metres before joining a dirt road on the right. Follow this dirt road east across flat fields ignoring a turn to the south (after 800m) and continue along it to a road. Turn right and follow the road into the village of **Tragó**. At a junction in the centre of the village turn east, continue along the road for 50 metres and then turn north along a trail running parallel to the **Río El Segre**. After 400 metres turn right over the bridge and follow the dirt road into **Oliana**.

Oliana is blighted by a busy road that runs along the length of the town and, among other things, takes traffic to and from Andorra. It does however have services and three hotels. Hotel Cal Petit is the best but located south of town and a couple of hundred metres along that busy road (973 470 449; **www.hotelcalpetit.es**). Hostal Victor is right in the middle of the town and has been run by the same family for three generations (973 470 010; **www.booking.com**) while Hotel Truc, which seems to be the most basic, is at the northern end (973 470 180).

STAGE 7
Oliana to Cambrils

Start	Carrer Josep Escaler, Oliana (430m)
Distance	13.5km
Ascent/Descent	960m/330m
Grade	4/4
Walking time	5hr 15min
Maximum altitude	1200m

The lack of accommodation beyond Cambrils necessitates a short stage, but it's an enjoyable one nonetheless, including some excellent views and a lot of ascent.

From where the GR1 enters Oliana head north along the main road and take the second right. Continue east to the end of the street (about 200m), turn left and head north for 300 metres where the road crosses a small stream and take the right-hand turn at a fork. Head northeast for 500 metres and turn right at a junction with a road. Follow the road east for 200 metres, turn left and head north for 100 metres then right and northeast onto a path. After 400 metres, join a road and continue east on the road for 1.9km. ◀

You will have been climbing gradually since you left Oliana.

Turn off the road and follow a path southeast around the top of a heavily-eroded gully. After 200 metres the path reaches a ridge and turns northeast. Continue along the rocky ridge for a kilometre passing the pretty little Romanesque **Ermita de Sant Just** on the way. The route then joins a dirt road, follows it along the south side of the ridge east for 400 metres, leaves it and continues on a lovely path up and along another ridge for 2km. It then joins a dirt road, turns right and follows it down a slope to another larger dirt road. Turn right onto this and follow it for 100 metres down to a road.

At the road turn left and follow the road up the hill for 400 metres before leaving it and continuing north

Ermita de Sant Just

along a path. Continue up the hill into open ground, reaching a road after a kilometre. ▸

Turn left onto the road.

An optional climb up a small hill to the left is suggested – a recommended place to take pictures (the **Mirador de Serra Seca**). To the southwest is a dramatic valley formed of two lines of cliffs, the Serra dels Obacs and Serra de les Canals. The views from the little hill are excellent but you can enjoy them without the climb a bit further along the route.

Follow the road north for 400 metres, leave it and continue along a lovely rocky path that runs parallel with the road for 1.4km. It then turns left and heads back down to the road (be careful not to go too far). Cross the road and follow a path over fields to the Romanesque church dedicated to Sant Mart de Cambrils and the ruins of a castle. Follow the road north to a campsite, cross the campsite to a road on the east side where you can find accommodation.

Opposite the junction is a metal installation depicting a cyclist celebrating the Tour de France which passed this point in 2010.

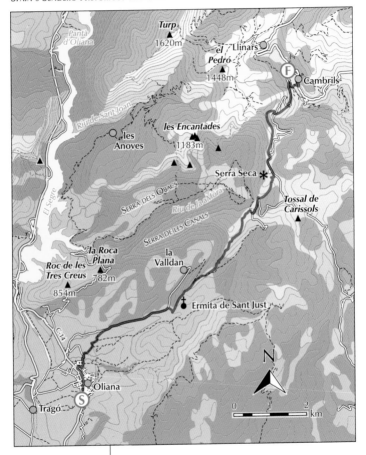

There are two places to stay – the Fonda Casa Nova (973 489014) and the Pensió Ca l'Agusta. Both places were open for lunch the last time I visited.

STAGE 8

*Cambrils to Sant Llorenç
de Morunys*

Start	Village centre, Cambrils (970m)
Distance	26km
Ascent/Descent	1090m/1300m
Grade	4/4
Walking time	9hr 20min
Maximum altitude	1470m

Stage 8 is both tough and a little frustrating. For the first 6km the route runs parallel to a new road (the route is probably following the old road) but with some much harder ascents and descents. This stretch is best avoided – either get a lift or walk on the new road to the turn-off down to Oriola (beware there is a short tunnel stretch) to turn a frustrating walk into an excellent one. You will need to pack your lunch.

Follow the road out of the village. Just around the first corner waymarks advise turning left for a parallel walk above the road but it's a nasty trail and best avoided.

After 2km the **official GR1** drops below the road but stays close to it for next 1.7km. Rejoining the road for about 200 metres the GR1 again leaves it and returns to parallel running. After 400 metres it drops steeply into a gully down a treacherous path and climbs out again on the other side.

Stay on the main road and rejoin the GR1 about 800 metres after a short tunnel (before the K26 marker on the road) by taking a right-hand turn down a dirt trail for about 100 metres to the GR1 waymark.

Continue east and then south along a dirt road for 700 metres and turn left onto a path (the dirt road continues south). Follow it past a farmstead (poor waymarking)

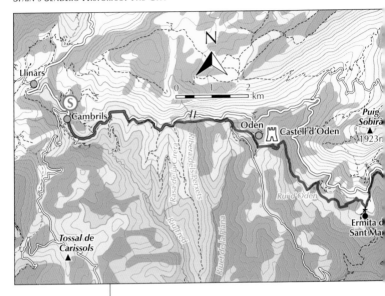

You have the option here of detouring to visit the ruins of the **Castell d'Oden** up across a field to the northwest.

to another dirt road to turn right and south. ◄ After a kilometre leave the dirt road and join a path heading east.

The path descends steeply into a gorge dropping 200m, and depending on the time of year you will have to take your boots off to cross the stream (the **Riu d'Odèn**) at the bottom. Follow the path southwest through trees on a gentle climb for 1.6km to a farmstead and a dirt road.

Follow the dirt road east past a chapel and head down a hill. At a fork take the left-hand turn and follow the dirt road up the hillside for 300 metres. At a bend in the road join a path heading east and follow it through

The path emerges near an interesting and suspicious-looking installation on a hillside – surrounded by wire and not marked on any maps.

trees for about 1.6km. ◄ Walk up to the farmstead and the **Ermita de Sant Marti**.

From the farmstead head north and continue for 900 metres past a turn-off to the right, a small reservoir, and a turn-off to the left. The route turns east once again running parallel with a road and a line of impressive cliffs. Cross a dirt road after 2.6km and head down into the tiny village of **Canalda**.

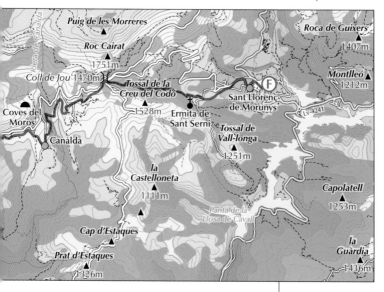

Head north out of Canalda, turn right after 300 metres and follow a well-marked path for 2.4km as it contours around two gullies. This is a particularly pleasant stretch of walking, with oak trees at the beginning and some spectacular little waterfalls. Watch out for the caves in the cliff face, the **Coves del Moros** (used by the Moors).

Coves del Moros

Emerging at the Coll de Jou (1470m) cross the main road and join an uncomfortable gullied rocky road heading steeply down the valley. After about 3km, by which time the going has improved, the route becomes a paved ancient path to the pretty Romanesque **Ermita de Sant Serni** and from there continues into **Sant Llorenç de Morunys**.

SANT LLORENÇ DE MORUNYS POPULATION 1038

Located a few kilometres south of the ski resort at Port del Comte, Sant Llorenç de Morunys, has its own attractions. The most important is the monastery built in the Romanesque-Lombard style in the 11th century. Inside is an elaborate and huge altar considered to be the most representative example of Catalan baroque art. The medieval walls of the town, including its four gateways, are intact.

The town has three hotels: Casa Joan, a fairly plain hotel but great value (provides an excellent sandwich) (973 492 055; **www.hostalcasajoan.com**); the Hostal Piteus (973 492 340; **www.hostalpiteus.com**) (both on Booking.com) and Pensió La Catalana (973 492 272).

STAGE 9

Sant Llorenç de Morunys to Sant Lleïr de la Vall d'Ora

Start	Car park, northern side of Sant Llorenç (840m)
Distance	24km
Ascent/Descent	1200m/1290m
Grade	4/4
Walking time	9hr
Maximum altitude	1400m

Stage 9 is a lovely walk, particularly the first and last sections. Although an uncharacteristic stretch of road-walking in the middle slightly spoils it, it does make the nine-hour walking time estimate easy to beat. The highlight is the Ermita de Sant Pere de Graudescales, a beautiful little chapel set in a stunning location. Take a bocadillo with you for sustenance.

Follow the main road, the Carrer de la Mercè, east down the hill. Just before the road turns south, turn left and head northeast. After 300 metres turn right onto a path, pass some agricultural buildings and continue for 500 metres down into a valley to the Hotel Monegal (609 773 209; www.monegal.com and www.booking.com).

Continue north and around some ugly derelict industrial buildings, turn right and head down (and briefly south) and across a river. Join a waymarked path and head east through trees before turning north. Follow the trail north, then east, for 2.2km to a hamlet at **Cal Calet** which features a small chapel, the Sant Lleïr de Casabella.

Continue east along a trail for 600 metres (crossing a little valley and then climbing) before taking a sharp left-hand turn onto a path. Follow a lovely path through trees as it climbs steeply joining another wider trail 600 metres later. Turn right and follow the trail south then north up the mountain, turning right onto a path after 500 metres.

Follow the path up through trees for 1.3km until it joins a dirt road on top of the mountain on open ground.

Since Cal Calet the route has climbed nearly 400m – a short diversion to the south of the route will take

Pantà de la Llosa de Cavall

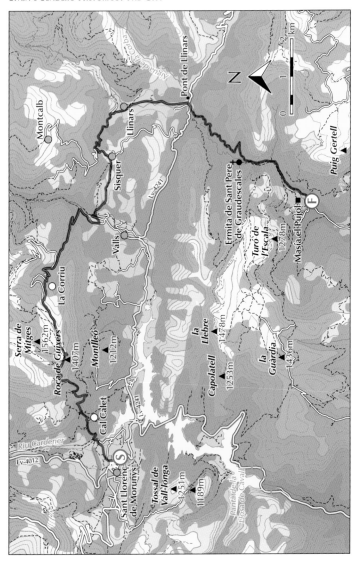

you to the edge of the cliff with great views south-west over the **Pantà de la Llosa de Cavall** (although a huge quarry to the south slightly spoils the effect).

Follow the dirt road east across an open meadow and ignore turns to the north up to summer grazing huts. Surprisingly the dirt road is suddenly metalled spoiling the walk somewhat. After a kilometre turn right (easily missed) and head down the hillside through trees rejoining the road near the hamlet **La Corriu**. Continue on for 4km.

Passing to the west of the field, on the other side of which is a river and three scattered houses, the road turns east and then south. Instead of turning south the GR1 heads north along an access road to the first of the three houses, crosses a bridge and into the grounds of the other two (very smart) houses. Follow a road towards the most northerly of the two and join a path immediately to its right. Stay on the path and continue to head east for 2km, crossing a low pass, arriving at a road just to the north of the hamlet **Sisquer**. ▸

Turn left onto the road and head north for 300 metres. Take a right turn onto an old trail, head east (ignoring a left-hand turn after 800m) and south into the lovely Vall Aigua d'Ora and continue for 1.5km to **Llinars**. The 'settlement' is very dispersed. Head south through scattered houses onto a road alongside the Valldora campsite and down to **Pont de Llinars**.

From the bridge follow a dirt track southwest taking the left-hand fork past a watermill after 400 metres. Follow the undulating dirt track for 3.1km (tough walking) where a short diversion visits the **Ermita de Sant Pere de Graudescales**.

Ermita de Sant Pere de Graudescales is a perfect Romanesque church in an exceptionally isolated setting at the bottom of a valley. Perhaps the most beautiful on the GR1, it was originally part of a Benedictine monastery and is now a national monument.

Enjoy views of Serra de Busa and the beautiful Romanesque church of Sant Esteve de Sisquer.

Monument to Wilfred the Hairy

After 1.5km the valley opens up and the route enters the scattered settlement of Sant Lleïr de la Vall d'Ora. Continue for 800 metres to the abandoned church, Ermita de Sant Lleïr. The Masía is located in the dispersed settlement on the western side of the valley away from the GR1. To get to it, turn right and then over a bridge and right again (passing the Ermita de Sant Llull) and then right onto a track up to the **Masía**. On the way, pass an interesting monument to Wilfred the Hairy (see the introduction to Section 7).

The largest property in the dispersed settlement is the Masia el Pujol which provides comfortable accommodation and food (973 299 045; **www.masiaelpujol. com**).

STAGE 10
Sant Lleïr de la Vall d'Ora to L'Espunyola

Start	Abandoned church, Ermita de Sant Lleïr (750m)
Distance	14.5km
Ascent/Descent	530m/510m
Grade	4/4
Walking time	6hr
Maximum altitude	1476m

Stage 10 includes the only bit of 'exposed' walking on the whole of GR1, a very short stretch where sure feet and a head for heights would be an advantage. It is a lovely walk, however, that includes one of best bits of ridge walking on the whole GR1. There is nowhere to eat on the way but the food at the hotel at the end is excellent.

From the abandoned church follow the GR1 waymarks east at the fork with the dirt road and then turn north (left) at a junction 200 metres later. The route now

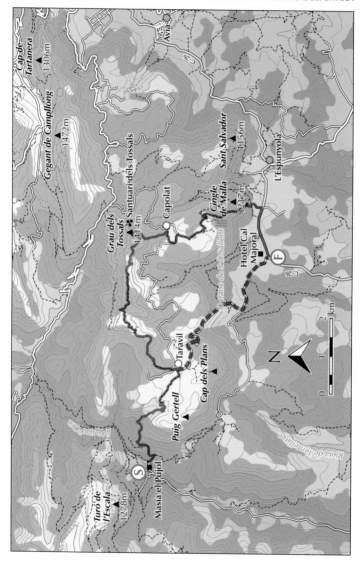

follows a combination of well-marked paths and dirt roads as it climbs gently east up the hillside for the next 1.8km.

After crossing a low ridge along a narrow path, the route turns south and climbs up the western side of valley along a dirt road. Reaching the end of the wooded valley (which could now be described as a gully) the route crosses it and zig-zigs its way up the eastern side through tangles of oak scrub. Taking the left-hand turn at a junction it follows a dirt trail for a kilometre until it emerges onto open pasture (which in May is a sea of dwarf daffodils). Eventually you will join a road near the scattered settlement at **Taravil**.

Variant exit to L'Espunyola avoiding exposure
If you are a nervous walker there is a local trail down to L'Espunyola from this point.

After 200 metres turn left at a junction with the road. As the road swings east towards a farmstead, leave it and follow a well-marked trail along a ridge for 600 metres and then turn right onto a path. The path follows a ridge, the Serra dels Tossals, for 5.3km with views to both north and south. The exposed stretch, about 10 metres with a significant drop to the south, is near the end and close to the ruins at **Santuari dels Tossals**.

Towards the end of the ridge walk the route swings north and starts to descend. After 400 metres it turns abruptly southwest and then south along a stunning trail for 1.3km down to pretty hamlet of **Capolat**. ◄

Set in the fields around Capolat is an unexpected set of modern art installations.

From the road to the west of the hamlet join a trail heading south. Follow it for a kilometre and then turn east and descend zig-zagging along a dirt road into a valley (past a farmstead) and then down the valley alongside a stream. The path then descends steeply down a cliff and past some waterfalls, the **Barranc de Salt Sallent**. About a kilometre after the waterfalls the trail hits a dirt road. Turn right here for the Hotel Restaurant **Cal Majoral**, and follow the dirt road down to the main road. The hotel is another kilometre to the west.

The Hotel Restaurant Cal Majoral is excellent and will provide or organise a lift to Gironella if you want to avoid the relatively dull final stage of this section (938 230 582; **www.calmajoral.com** and **www.booking. com**).

Barranc de Salt Sallent

STAGE 11
L'Espunyola to Gironella

Start	Hotel Cal Majoral, L'Espunyola (800m)
Distance	20.5km
Ascent/Descent	660m/310m
Grade	2/4
Walking time	5hr 30min
Maximum altitude	500m

This last stage crosses the valley to Gironella. It's short and after the dramatic scenery of the last few days, just a little dull. For a mid-trip break stop at Avià.

Take the main road east from the hotel into L'Espunyola. (Hitching may be a possibility.) From the junction in the centre of the village, head southeast across an open patch of ground and join a dirt road heading south through buildings. After 50 metres the dirt road turns east and heads into open countryside. Follow it east for 500 metres, then turn south past a house and along a path through woods to join another dirt road after 400 metres. Head east taking a right fork after 600 metres and continue southeast for another 500 metres. Ignore a turn to the right and continue southeast for 600 metres (ignoring turns to the right and then to the left).

Passing a farmstead continue east along a dirt road for a kilometre and then leave the road, turning left, and follow a path for 300 metres before re-joining a dirt road. Turn left, follow the dirt road for 600 metres to a junction and turn right. Continue south then east, passing a couple of farmsteads, for a kilometre until you reach a junction with another dirt trail. Turn right, continue north along the trail for 600 metres, cross a junction, and continue north for another 1.7km, to a road and the southern outskirts of **Avià**. ◄

Avià has a coffee bar and other services but there is not much in the small town to encourage a longer stay.

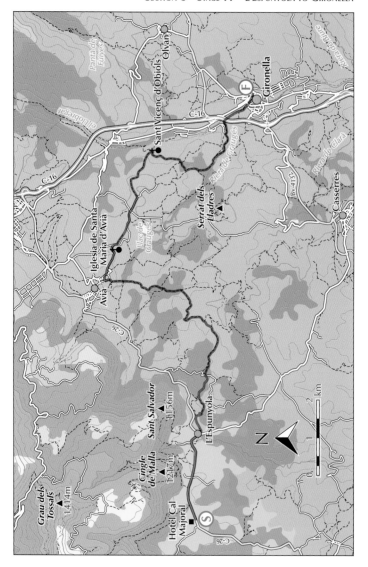

Joining the road the GR1 heads north, takes the first right, then takes another right, then a left (to visit the village church) and continues on a road out of the town.

Continue southeast along the road for 600 metres to a little Romanesque chapel (**Iglesia de Santa Maria d'Avià**), and continue east to join a road. Cross the road and continue southeast along a dirt trail for 500 metres to rejoin the road. Follow the road southeast for 800 metres passing through a small settlement and a junction with another road, then turn left onto a minor access road. Follow the road east and then southeast for 1.6km to **Sant Vicenç d'Obiols**.

> **Sant Vicenç d'Obiols** is a particularly beautiful Romanesque church. Some elements are possibly pre-Romanesque (Visigothic) and there is documentary evidence that the building existed in the mid-9th century. It has a picturesque location above the **Río El Llobregat** to the east.

From the church follow a dirt road west and then south for a kilometre. Ignore turns to the north and south and continue southwest for another 300 metres, turning left and heading south at a junction. Continue south past buildings for a kilometre, and take a right fork onto a path. Follow a path near a stream south and then east for a kilometre, join a dirt road and head east underneath the motorway and south into **Gironella**.

GIRONELLA POPULATION 5063

Gironella is a significant town but doesn't have a lot by way of attractions. The old part of the town sits on a hill on the eastern side of the town and has a large neo-Gothic church on top. The town straddles the Río El Llobregat.

There are two hotels, the tiny but well-located Hostal 1888 (**www.booking.com**) and the larger Hotel L'Oreneta De Gironella (38 228 548; **www.hotel-oreneta. com**) which is modern and functional but not interesting and located well to the south of the town centre.

242

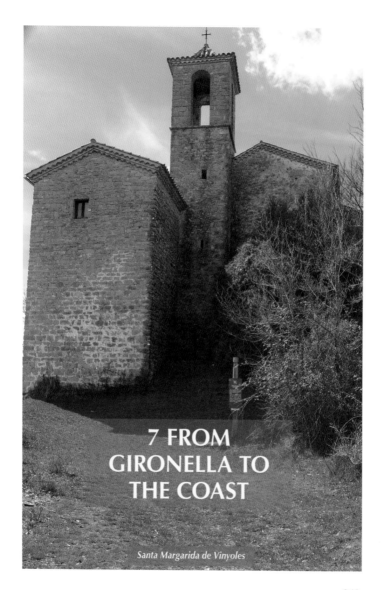

7 FROM GIRONELLA TO THE COAST

Santa Margarida de Vinyoles

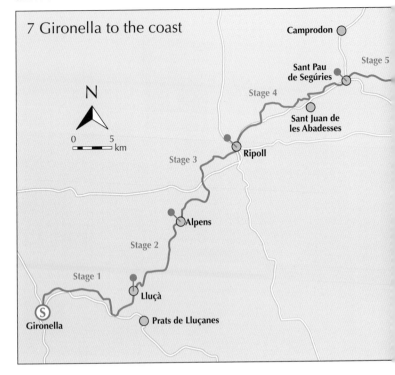

7 Gironella to the coast

Camprodon

Stage 5

Sant Pau
de Segúries

Stage 4

Sant Juan de
les Abadesses

N

0   5
━━━━━ km

Stage 3

Ripoll

Alpens

Stage 2

Stage 1

Lluçà

Prats de Lluçanes

Gironella

If you have walked all the way from Puerto de Tarna your emotions at this point will probably be mixed. With the end in 'in sight' you will be excited about finishing and amazed that you have got this far – last laps however are notoriously tough and another 191km could still feel impossibly far. Fear not: after what has been accomplished this last section is a breeze, only 5000m of climb in total and two days of easy walking across the coastal plain, a chance to dip your toes in the Mediterranean and then home.

From a historical perspective the land you will walk through was particularly rich and one where the second great character of the Marca Hispánica (after Sancho the Great) left his mark.

Essentially ruling on behalf of his Carolingian patrons, Wilfred the Hairy started his 'reign' with the county of Urgell (one of the constituent units of the Marca Hispánica) and then added

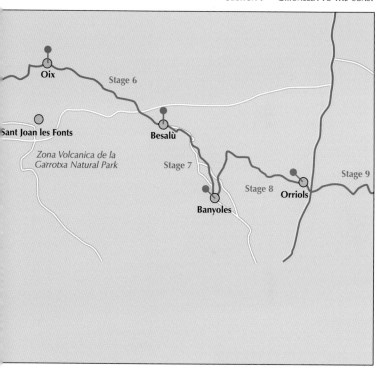

Cerdanya, Barcelona, Girona, Besalú, and Ausana. Such was his success that on his death in 897 his territories passed to his son establishing a dynasty. Personal characteristics, by the way, were at this time often used to name leaders. As well as Wilfred the Hairy there was a Charles the Bald (actually very hairy), a Charles the Simple and a Lothar the Lame.

Wilfred the Hairy was a great builder and Romanesque buildings and settlements on this part of the trail are typically a hundred years older than elsewhere. They were used to accommodate a religious advance guard (monks and nuns) used to establish geographic dominance. The GR1 visits three such sites – Ripoll, Sant Joan de les Abadesses and Besalú.

The route passes through two distinct types of scenery. The first half continues with the pre-Pyrenean theme of the last three stages, although despite getting within a few kilometres of the French border

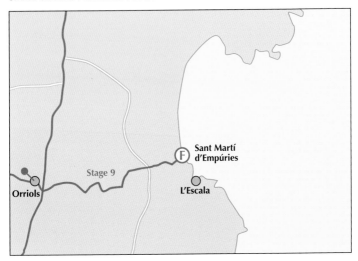

the mountains are not so high. The second half crosses the coastal plain on the final approach to the Mediterranean.

ACCESS AND ACCOMMODATION

The GR1 reaches the sea at Sant Martí d'Empúries, about a kilometre to the north of the resort of L'Escala looking out into the beautiful Bay of Roses. Buses from the town (www.grup sarbus.com) provide access to the nearest train station, Flaçà, or direct access to Girona or Barcelona airports.

Accommodation is good and plenty of choices en route mean you don't need to leave the trail at the end of the day.

SECTION 7: KEY INFORMATION	
Distance	191km
Total ascent	4770m
Total descent	5090m
Alternative schedule	Oix is a good base for walks into L'Alta Garrotxa Natural Park and a good candidate for an extra day if time allows.

STAGE 1

Gironella to Lluçà

Start	Santa Eulàlia (old church), Gironella (500m)
Distance	30.5km
Ascent/Descent	710m/440m
Grade	3/3
Walking time	9hr
Maximum altitude	830m

Stage 1 is a long stage but with easy walking through pleasant countryside. There is a good place to stop for lunch. The worst bit is the exit from Gironella and if you want a shorter day take a taxi to Olvan.

From the large church head north to the main road. Follow it north, turn left after 400 metres and then, after a few metres, right. Continue north for 1.7km into open countryside, over a bridge across a new road and to a new and empty industrial estate. Turn east and continue east-northeast for 2km to the village of **Olvan**, ignoring a junction about 500 metres before the village.

> **Olvan** is an attractive little town with several bars and restaurants, but unfortunately no accommodation. The church, originally Romanesque, has been heavily restored.

From the centre of town head south along the main road, turn east alongside a building and a field and continue along a dirt road for 700 metres to a junction with a road. Turn right at the junction onto the road and then left again onto a dirt road and continue east. After 200 metres leave the dirt road and join a path, follow it for 400 metres and cross a road. Follow the path for another 400 metres then rejoin the road, turn north, cross it and join a dirt road heading east through a farmstead. ▶

The landscape is now distinctively barren with large patches of flat exposed rock and just an occasional piece of cultivated land.

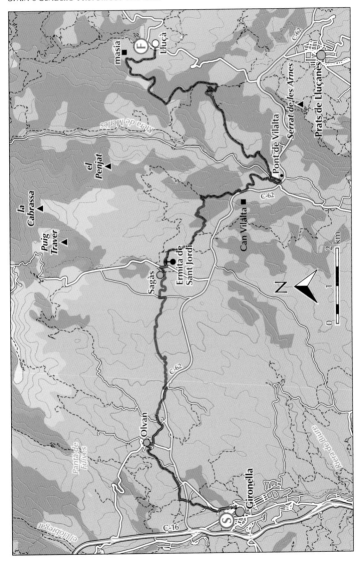

Head east past the farmstead and down into a rocky valley. The waymarks at this point may be hard to spot but on crossing the river the route heads northeast and then follows a slight valley east. The path then becomes more obvious and after 600 metres turns right, drops down to a dirt road and continues east-southeast to a farmstead.

From the farmstead continue east for 500 metres, turn left onto a minor road, head north for 200 metres and then turn right onto a path heading east. Follow the path east for 500 metres and turn left onto a dirt road. Head north along it for 50 metres, turn right and head east along a path into **Sagàs**.

Sagàs is a tiny but stunning little village. It is dominated by an early 11th-century church dedicated to Sant Andreu and regarded as one of the best examples of Catalan Romanesque architecture.

To the northwest of the village is a derelict chapel dedicated to St Margarida which is even older – late 10th century – and includes features

Sant Andreu at Sagàs

which are considered to be pre-Romanesque. The GR1 intersects the GR38 which, at this point, is being followed by the E4 heading up from Tarifa (near Gibraltar) and continuing all the way through Europe to Greece.

Turn south along the main road towards a chapel (**Ermita de Sant Jordi**) and turn east along a dirt road. ◄

For the next 3km take care as the GR1 plots a complex course across fields and it's easy to miss a turning.

Continue east past a farmstead reaching a junction after 500 metres. Turn right, head south and southeast, through fields, for a kilometre to a junction with a dirt road. Turn right, then left and head southeast past a farmstead. 200 metres from the farmstead turn left off the dirt trail and follow a path east across a field. Turn right at the other side and head southeast alongside the edge of a wood. After 100 metres turn left and follow a dirt road for 150 metres heading northeast.

Leave the dirt road and continue northeast along a path until it joins another dirt road 200 metres later. Turn right, head south for 50 metres, leave the dirt road and follow a path heading southeast for 500 metres until it joins a dirt road. Follow the dirt road northeast turning south at a junction with another dirt road after 200 metres. Head south past a pig farm for 1.3km until the route reaches a road.

Head southeast along the road and turn left after about 100 metres. Follow a dirt road over a bridge, turn right and then take the first left past farm buildings. To the south is a fairly grand farmstead (**Can Vilalta**) and a chapel (Ermita de la Santissima Trinitat). Head east for 300 metres along a dirt road and turn south. Here the waymarks are again hard to follow, possibly removed, but the route heads directly south through a farmstead (a rural tourism centre with a very pretty watermill, Molí de Vilalta) down to the road and a bridge, the **Pont de Vilalta**. ◄

Next to the bridge is a small hotel, Sant Cristòfol, which serves excellent food, and is a great place for a lunch stop (938 250 525).

Turn left off the road (to the left-hand side of the hotel) and head north along a dirt road for 1.2km. Take a left-hand turn and continue north and then northeast for 3.8km. Just before it reaches a small farmstead the route leaves the dirt road and heads east along another dirt road. Continue east for 600 metres, ignore a turn to the north, and go northeast for 1.5km meandering around fields to a junction with a minor road.

Head north along the road and take a right-hand fork after 800 metres. Continue north (now along a dirt road) for 1.7km to a farmstead, turn right and head east. Follow the road as it swings to the north (ignore a turn to the east) and take a right-hand fork after 800 metres. Follow the road as it turns east, ignore a turn to the north and continue around the valley to a large and very beautiful **farmstead** – a 'masia'.

> The '**masia**' is a distinct feature of Catalonia and you will see a number of them on the remainder of the walk. They are enormous farmhouses associated with significant livestock farms and are often very old and based on Roman villas. They are usually two-storey buildings with the ground floor used for farming purposes and the first floor for occupation by a large extended family.

Just before the masia turn right and head south along a path. After 800 metres turn east and head into **Lluçà**.

LLUÇÀ POPULATION <20

Lluçà, a tiny scattering of houses, nestles below the ruins of the Castell de Lluçà which towers above it on a hill. Near the castle and up from the GR1 sits a pretty Romanesque chapel dedicated to St Vincent and in the village there is the larger Monasteri de Santa María de Lluçà famous for its murals and cloisters. Some of the buildings date back to the 9th century and were constructed as part of Wilfred the Hairy's repopulation of the area.

The little hostal, the Hostal Fonda (La Primitiva), is opposite the church, and is particularly comfortable (628 631 246; **www.fondalaprimitiva.com**).

STAGE 2
Lluçà to Alpens

Start	Hostal Fonda, Lluçà (730m)
Distance	14km
Ascent/Descent	530m/370m
Grade	4/4
Walking time	4hr 40min
Maximum altitude	900m

This is a short and easy stage through pretty countryside with some excellent views of the Pyrenees. Watch out for views of El Pedraforca (2506m), a distinct forked mountain visible at various points towards the northeast. If you want a challenge consider combining today with the next stage where a long downhill concrete road makes the estimated time easy to beat.

The views from this point to the Pyrenees are excellent. ◄

Follow the road north and take a left turn onto a dirt road. After 200 metres at a junction with another dirt road take a right-hand fork and continue north, past a fortified farmstead (**El Castell**). ◄

After a kilometre take a right-hand turn off the dirt road onto a path and head east through trees before swinging north again after a few metres. Continue north-northeast, crossing meadows at one point, for 850 metres to a dirt road (watching out for the views back to the castle above Lluçà). Turn right onto the dirt road and follow it down along a winding route (ignoring a left-hand turn after 300m) for a kilometre.

Turn right onto a path, head down to a dirt road at the bottom of a valley (where there is a water mill just to south) and head east past a farmstead onto a road. As the road leaves the settlement heading south take a sharp left turn up past some farm buildings and onto a dirt road. Continue east along the dirt road for 1.7km passing through the little settlement of **Molí de Puig-oriol** and into the village of **Santa Eulàlia de Puig-oriol** (no services).

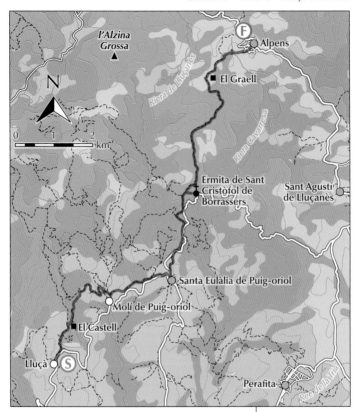

Leave the road as it heads northwest out of the village, take a right turn onto a path and follow it north for 500 metres until it joins the road again. Cross the road and continue along an old transhumance route north (parallel with the road below to the east) for a kilometre. After passing farm buildings take a right-hand turn at a junction with another dirt road.

After 700 metres you can make a short detour up to the **Ermita de Sant Cristòfol de Borrassers**.

The views of the Pyrenees from El Castell north of Lluçà

Head north for 800 metres, ignore forks to the right and left and continue north, then east, for 1.3km. Ignore a turn to the right and continue north for another 1.3km, then take a left fork passing a very impressive agricultural building at **El Graell** and follow the route round as it swings east into **Alpens**.

ALPENS POPULATION 304

Alpens is a small town and the location for one of the key battles of the Carlist war on 9 July 1873. The large Gothic church, dedicated to Santa Maria, has been heavily restored and only the tower is original (the church was damaged by fire during the Carlist war).

There are a few shops, a bar, restaurant and accommodation at the Fonda Alpens (93 8578143) and a casa rural at Cal Miquel (686 633 0540). Watch out for the work of a local ironmonger – there are some particularly impressive door fittings.

STAGE 3

Alpens to Ripoll

Start	Town centre church, Alpens (880m)
Distance	21.5km
Ascent/Descent	860m/1010m
Grade	3/4
Walking time	7hr 40min
Maximum altitude	1120m

Stage 3 is another lovely easy walk through pleasant countryside. After an initial climb there is a good ridge with occasional views through trees followed by a long tramp down a concrete road through cattle country. The final third of the walk, down a charming valley, includes some more excellent examples of the traditional Catalonian masias. There is nowhere on the way for lunch so take a picnic.

Following the street on the north side of the church northeast through the town to the main road, turn right (just past some iron statues) and head northeast for 150 metres. Turn west onto a dirt road and follow it as it swings to the north for 1.8km and climbs up a valley. Leave the dirt road and follow a path steeply up a hill, heading east for 1.3km, and cross a dirt road.

Follow the path up and east along a lovely wooded ridge reaching a church, **Santa Margarida de Vinyoles**, after 1.1km.

The views to the north from the church across the **Serra de Santa Margarida de Vinyoles** are excellent. The church itself is Romanesque in origin but heavily restored.

Heading east down from the church, turn left off the dirt road and follow a path into trees on the northern side

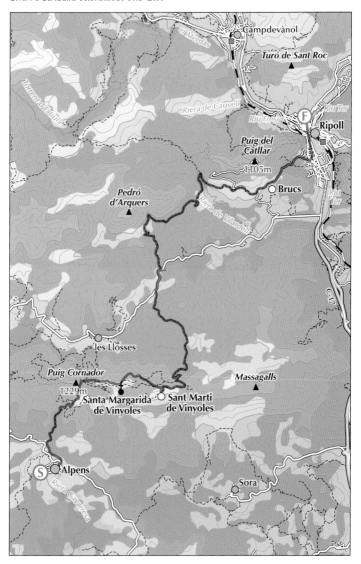

Fortified manor house at Sant Marti de Vinyoles

of the ridge. The path turns into a dirt road and, 1.2km from the church, takes a right fork and continues south-east to the tiny hamlet of **Sant Marti de Vinyoles**.

> **Sant Marti de Vinyoles** is very picturesque with a fortified 14th-century manor house with a tower at the western end of the village and a Romanesque church built onto a house at the eastern end.

From Sant Marti de Vinyoles the route joins a concrete road and follows it relentlessly north for the next 5km. At the bottom it joins another road and continues north for 600 metres before turning left and joining a forest trail.

Continue north up a valley for 1.6km. After zigzagging up through trees follow the dirt trail into open countryside and turn east, climbing over a pass. There are some excellent examples of masia farmsteads scattered around the lovely upland valley. Continue east, descending all the time, for 3.5km. At the scattered settlement of **Brucs** the route leaves the road and follows a dirt trail east-northeast, continuing for another 2km to **Ripoll**.

Masia amidst ancient terracing

RIPOLL POPULATION 10,094

Ripoll sits in a tight valley at the confluence of the Riu Ter and its tributary Freser. The most important building, almost the foundation of the town itself, is the monastery of Santa Maria de Ripoll. The monastery was founded by Wilfred the Hairy in 880AD and was key to the repopulation of the whole area. The main church can be dated back to 935 and the complex was in continuous use as a monastery until 1835 after which it fell into disrepair. The current building, the church and its cloister, is a result of 19th-century restoration work. Perhaps the most important feature is the main entrance built in the middle of the 12th century. With its profusion of Old Testament figures, it is regarded as the most important piece of Romanesque Catalan sculpture.

Ripoll has the full range of services including four hotels: La Trobada (972 702 353; www.latrobadahotel.com and www.booking.com), modern and comfortable and located near the monastery; the Cal la Paula (972 700 011; www.elripolles.com); the Solana de Ter (972 701 062; www.solanadelter.com) and the Hostal del Ripollés (972 700 215; www.hostaldelripolles.com). In terms of public transport Ripoll is well connected with a direct train service to Barcelona.

STAGE 4

Ripoll to Sant Pau de Segúries

Start	Monastery of Santa Maria, Ripoll (700m)
Distance	25km
Ascent/Descent	970m/740m
Grade	3/4
Walking time	8hr 15min
Maximum altitude	950m

Stage 4 is an easy walk and, apart from an excursion up a side valley, follows the main valley heading east from Ripoll. St Joan de les Abadesses is a good place to stop for lunch.

From the eastern side of the monastery join the Carrer del Dr Raguer, head north and continue in the same direction into the Carreterra de Sant Joan. After 700 metres join a footpath and follow it for 2.3km to the edge of town and a roundabout. Cross over the roundabout and continue parallel to the road for 2.5km before turning north, away from the valley, along a road for 400 metres.

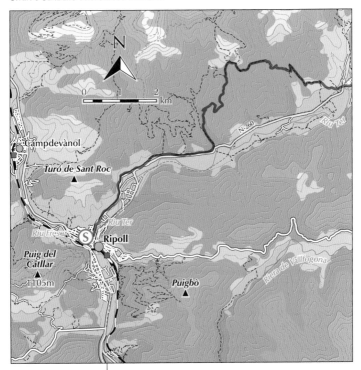

Leave the road and follow a wooded path on a meandering route up the valley side. After 2.7km, passing some scattered dwellings on the way, the route emerges at a road and turns right. Follow the road north then east and turn right (after 600m) onto a dirt road. Follow this on a steep descent down to a farmstead. Continuing east follow a path down into a valley, up the other side and join a dirt road as it heads north into another valley. Turn right at a junction with another dirt road at the bottom of the valley and follow it for 1.2km to the tiny settlement of Serra del Pradell. Turn left at the road in the village and follow the path along a field boundary southeast to the road and **Sant Joan de les Abadesses**.

SANT JOAN DE LES ABADESSES POPULATION 3469

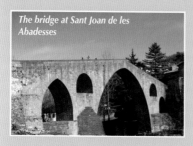
The bridge at Sant Joan de les Abadesses

Sant Joan de les Abadesses is another town whose origins can be traced back to Wilfred the Hairy and his founding of a nunnery here in 887AD (closed in 1017 when the nuns where accused of debauchery). The most important building is the Monastery of Sant Joan de les Abadesses that dates back to the 12th century, although much of the original building was destroyed by a strong earthquake in 1428. The bridge which dominates the centre of town also had a troubled past with the original one destroyed by the earthquake and the second one destroyed by retreating Republicans in the civil war. There are some remains of the original town walls including one of the towers.

There is accommodation at the Can Janpere (972 720 077; www.areljanpere.com and www.booking.com) and the youth hostel in a recently converted railway station (972 720 495; www.santjoandelesabadesses.cat).

The GR1 doesn't cross the river into the old part of town but continues east on the river's northern side.

Turn left immediately before crossing the old bridge and head east to join the road. Follow the road past the recently converted railway station and turn right along the old railway line. After 250 metres turn right onto a dirt road and continue east for 2km, ignoring turn-offs to the north and south. Turn sharp left and head north for 700 metres joining a dirt road as it crosses a river and turns east-southeast. After 800 metres the path reaches a bridge and doesn't cross it but turns right along the north bank, passing another river bridge 2km later. 200 metres from the bridge it leaves the dirt road (which continues up the hill) and joins a path heading east and follows it for 3.1km before joining a road (after a frustrating meander at the end). The road takes you into **Sant Pau de Segúries** in the middle of the Vall de Camprodón.

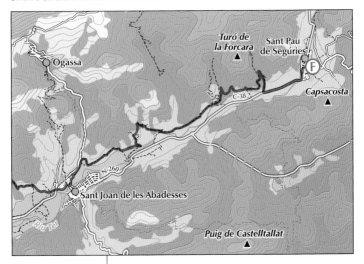

There is not much left of the original Sant Pau de Segúries but there are at least two bars and other services including cashpoints. Accommodation is available in the Hostal El Roures (972 747 000; **www.elsroures. com** and **www.booking.com**), part of a campsite to the east of the town.

STAGE 5

Sant Pau de Segúries to Oix

Start	Main road on the eastern side of Sant Pau at Carrer Guardia (850m)
Distance	19.5km
Ascent/Descent	690m/1130m
Grade	4/4
Walking time	7hr
Maximum altitude	920m

Stage 5 passes through the middle of the L'Alta Garrotxa Natural Park famous for its conical mountains – the remains of ancient volcanoes. After a relatively busy valley on the previous stage it is surprisingly remote. Despite being so close to the Pyrenees it's an easy walk, essentially through deciduous woodland along valley sides. The hotel at the end in Oix is especially welcoming and a great place to stop for a late and lengthy Spanish lunch.

Start by heading east from the junction along the Avenida El Mariner. After passing the northern side of a campsite continue along a dirt road between fields for 300 metres. Turn left at a junction, past an upmarket holiday centre (which does not offer single-night accommodation) and follow the road east for 1.2km. Leave the road as it turns sharply west and continue east down to rejoin the road. (The route takes a strange course just before reaching the road.)

Continue along the road for 1.3km, leaving it to join a path as it turns to the west. Follow the path southeast across the valley joining a dirt road after 1.4km. Continue along the dirt road east through trees for 4km to a lovely old stone farmstead at **Llongarriu** (being restored on my last visit) and the beautiful Romanesque church Ermita de la Mare de Deu dels Angels. Heading northeast the path drops down to a road and the **Hostal Vall de la Bac** (not currently open).

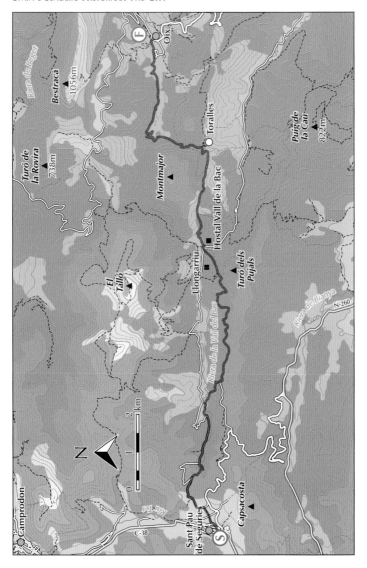

Pont Romá d'Oix

Cross the road and follow a dirt road east up through trees for 200 metres. As the dirt road swings to the north, leave it and join a forest trail heading east. After 3km the trail turns north and heads into an opening, near the tiny settlement of **Toralles** (home to a riding school) with the Romanesque church of Sant Martí.

Continue north along a trail for 2.5km, and just before a large masia the dirt road becomes a metalled one. Follow the road southeast along the valley for 3km into **Oix**.

OIX POPULATION 102

Oix is a lovely little mountain village at the bottom of a deep valley – look out for the high arched medieval bridge Pont Romá d'Oix. The bridge, according to legend, was used by the local baron to parade women about to be married and upon which he would decide whether to exercise his medieval 'derecho de pernada' or 'droit de seigneur' privilege.

The Hostal de la Rovira provides excellent food and accommodation in a carefully restored 15th-century building (972 294 347; **www.hostaldelarovira.es** and **www.booking.com**).

STAGE 6
Oix to Besalú

Start	Hostal de la Rovira, Oix (400m)
Distance	21km
Ascent/Descent	370m/620m
Grade	3/4
Walking time	6hr 40min
Maximum altitude	630m

Today you say goodbye to the mountains and start the descent onto the coastal plain. Besalú is an amazing place with lots to see so it's worth trying to get there early.

The Pont del Llierca

Follow the main road (just to the south of the hotel) south and then east across the valley for 700 metres. Turn left

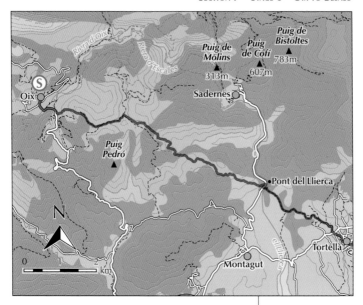

onto a forest path and climb up along the path for 1.7km to join a dirt road. Follow the dirt road east for 700 metres (ignoring a turn to the south after 200m) and take a sharp turn south onto a path (easily missed if the weather isn't good). Follow the path southeast down into a valley. After 1.6km the path joins a dirt road and continues southeast for 4km (ignoring a turn to the southwest after 1km) to the beautiful **Pont del Llierca**.

> Perhaps the best of a number of stunning bridges along the GR1, the very slender, single arch of **Pont del Llierca** towers 28m over el Llierca. It's 52 metres long, 3 metres wide and was a commercial proposition when it was built in the 14th century.

Cross the bridge and continue southeast along a dirt road for 3km (ignoring a turn to the south after 900m) into the little town of **Tortellà**.

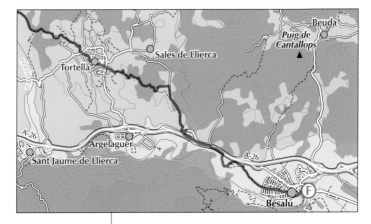

Tortellà is a small town with a range of services including bars and cashpoints. Accommodation is available at the Hostal Alta Garrotxa (972 287 878; www.hotelaltagarrotxa.com and www.booking.com).

From the main square in the town centre, take the street midway along its eastern side, head east and continue along the north side of a public park to a main road. Cross the main road and continue for 300 metres to where the route leaves the road and follows a dirt road heading down to buildings. After 50 metres or so leave the dirt road and continue along a path heading east. The path zig-zags its way eastwards joining a dirt road after 400 metres. Follow the dirt road for 500 metres leaving it as it turns south to join another path. Head east through trees for 600 metres to a dirt road near a chapel (Sant Andreu). Head north and then east to a junction (500 metres) and then head south for 1.7km to an access road just to the north of an incredibly busy dual carriageway.

The official route travels down to the dual carriageway, along its northern side and then crosses it 800 metres later. ◄ The safer option, perhaps, involves staying on the access road, heading east over the old bridge,

Waymarks are few are far between. (They usually are when the news is bad.)

268

The Monastery of San Pedro

taking the first left on a maintenance road underneath the dual carriageway, and then following it east for a kilometre. (There is a maintenance road to the south.)

Once you are across and you're 800 metres along on the south side of the dual carriageway, take a right turn south, drop into the valley, and follow a dirt road east into **Besalú**.

BESALÚ POPULATION 2427

Besalú competes with Sos del Rey Católico for the title of the best-preserved medieval town on the GR1. Although not as significant historically, it has a bigger and better collection of ancient Romanesque buildings. Already a prosperous town by the end of the 9th century it owed its success as a market town to its location at the point where the mountains meet the plain. This wealth financed construction, including the bridge over the Río Fluvià complete with fortified towers. Inside the town walls is a maze of narrow arcaded streets, including a Jewish quarter with its restored *mikveh*, a small bath used for purification rituals, and a synagogue dating back to the 11th century. The most important religious building is the Monastery of San Pedro, right in the heart of the town facing a lovely restaurant-lined square. The monastery was founded in 977AD and the church consecrated in 1003 with building continuing for the next 150 years.

The town has all the usual services and lots of accommodation. The Hotel3Arcs (972 591 678; www.hotel3arcs.com and www.booking.com) has a particularly good location.

STAGE 7
Besalú to Banyoles

Start	Medieval bridge, Besalú (140m)
Distance	14.5km
Ascent/Descent	250m/290m
Grade	2/3
Walking time	4hr 10min
Maximum altitude	190m

This short and easy stage is included because of the difficulty in finding accommodation within a day's walk of Besalú. You could tag it onto the last stage or miss it out altogether by using the frequent bus service connecting the two towns. To be honest, it's not a great walk.

Cross Besalú's amazing bridge and the car park immediately to the south of it and join the path up the hill. The path swings east and then heads southeast for a kilometre. Ignore the first and second left turns but take the third one and head down to the main Banyoles road. Turn right onto the road, follow it south for 100 metres and turn right onto a dirt road.

After 100 metres take a right-hand turn and head southeast and uphill for 400 metres where the dirt road splits. Take the left-hand fork and continue south for 3km (ignoring turns to the east and west), dropping down into the valley and joining up again with the road to Banyoles.

Once the main road is reached follow it along a dirt road on its western side for 400 metres and turn left through a tunnel underneath the road (opposite some large gates). Follow the dirt road up the hill for 150 metres, turn right and head south along a path through trees into **Serinyà**.

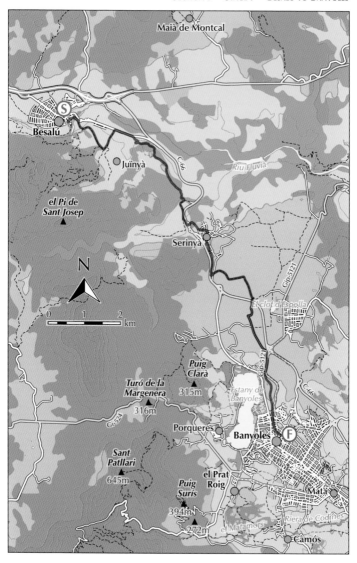

Serinya has a café, a stop for a bus to Banyoles, and some prehistoric caves which some claim are among the best of their kind in Europe.

From the 12th-century church head south and back towards the main road. The route runs parallel with road along a path for about 800 metres before turning east and heading up through trees. After 600 metres it joins a dirt road, turns left and continues east to a junction where it turns south. After 700 metres it crosses a bridge over the Banyoles road. From the other side of the bridge it continues south, joining the Banyoles road after 1.8km. Follow the road south for 400 metres and then turn right onto a dirt road running above and parallel to the main road into **Banyoles**.

BANYOLES POPULATION 17,309

Banyoles is a prosperous tourist town located alongside the largest natural lake in Spain and was the venue for the rowing competitions during the Barcelona Olympics. A large town, it has a historic centre dating back to the 9th century. Particularly important, and a national monument, is the monastery of St Stephen where the first Benedictine foundation was established between 801 and 820AD. The other important religious building is the 14th-century Gothic church dedicated to Santa Maria Turers.

There are lots of hotels – well located although a bit pricey is the Ca L'Arpa (972 572 353; **www.calarpa.com** and **www.booking.com**).

STAGE 8

Banyoles to Orriols

Start	Monastery of St Stephen, Banyoles (170m)
Distance	21km
Ascent/Descent	250m/250m
Grade	3/3
Walking time	5hr 40min
Maximum altitude	260m

Stage 8 is the beginning of the end and the first of two days of easy walking across the flat coastal plain. The main challenge is finding the right way out of Banyoles. There is nowhere to eat on the way so pack a picnic.

From the monastery head north for 300 metres along the Cami Fondo, over a junction, and north along the Carreterra Figueroles. Turn left and continue along a large road for 500 metres, turning left onto an access

On the coastal plain

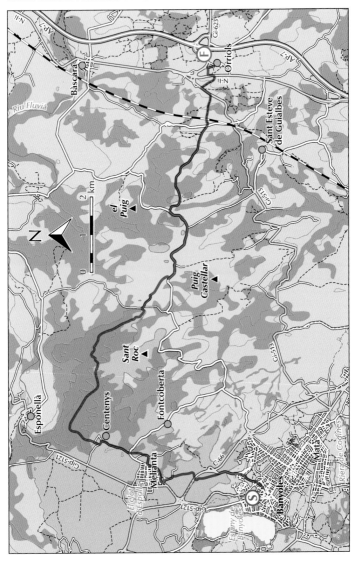

road. Follow it for 700 metres and turn right over a bridge crossing a major road. Continue east for 100 metres then turn left at a junction. Follow the dirt road for 900 metres, northwest, to **Melianta**, a housing suburb of Banyoles.

Turn right at the main road on the southern edge of the settlement, and after 100 metres take the second left back to the east edge of the settlement. Follow the road northeast for 500 metres, turn right at a roundabout and after 250 metres turn left. Continue north for 1.4km to a small village, **Centenys**, which has a fine Romanesque church (Sant Iscle).

Turn left at the southern edge of the village, then right and follow a dirt road north for a kilometre. Turn right at a junction with another dirt road and continue east-south-east for 4.5km. After crossing a junction with another dirt road continue in the same direction for another 1.2km. Turn right and then left again, after 50 metres, onto a road and follow this road east for 2.5km. Turn right (leaving the road which at this point is heading north) and head east along a dirt track. Follow the dirt track east for 2.8km, cross a road (the railway line on the map is in a tunnel at this point), and continue east for another 900 metres to another road. Head north along the road for 300 metres and then turn right and head southeast into **Orriols** crossing a larger road on the way.

Although Orriols has a pretty Romanesque church (San Ginés), the main attraction is a smart hotel (relatively expensive) in the converted castle – L'Odissea de L'Empordà (972 551 718; **www.odissea-emporda. com**). Only one more day to go so it's a great opportunity for a bit of indulgence but if you have run out of money then press onto Camallera where the hotel is a lot cheaper.

STAGE 9

Orriols to Sant Martí d'Empúries

Start	L'Odissea de L'Empordà hotel, Orriols (150m)
Distance	23km
Ascent/Descent	190m/220m
Grade	4/4
Walking time	6hr 15min
Maximum altitude	173m

This is the last day and if you're lucky with the weather it's an excellent walk, combining views of the Pyrenees to the north and the stunning Gulf of Roses to the east. There are places to stop for lunch on what is a short and easy last stage.

From the hotel head southeast through narrow streets to a marked path on the southeast edge of the village and follow it across fields. After a kilometre turn east and follow the route underneath the **motorway**. Continue east-northeast along a path that drops down through trees into a little valley and heads towards a road running east–west in just over 3km. Bypassing the village of **Llampaies** to the north, join the road and continue east for 800 metres, leave the road and head down a dirt track into the village of **Camallera**.

> **Camallera** is a small town in the middle of the coastal plain with accommodation and a restaurant (under separate management) at the Pension L'Avi Pep (972 794 056; www.lavipep.com and www.booking.com). There is also a bar, other shops and a railway station.

Cross the road bridge over the railway line and, on the other side, leave the road and join a dirt track heading southeast. Continue for 1.5km into the little village of **Pins**.

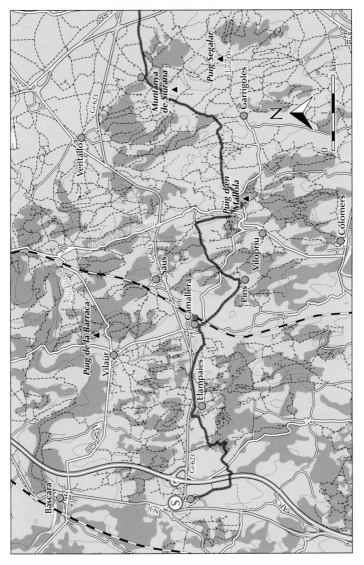

Mosaic at Sant Martí d'Empúries

Head north-northeast for 600 metres crossing another dirt track on the way. Cross a road, continue northeast (crossing another junction) through a pleasant mix of fields and woodland and climb to a low ridge. On the ridge, and after 1.6km, turn south and continue along a boundary between woodland and fields for another kilometre. After passing a house, turn east. Cross a road and continue southeast turning left onto another road. Follow the road east for 300 metres and turn left off the road onto a dirt track. Continue east along the track, ignoring several turns to the north and south, for 2.8km. Turn left as the main track continues east and head northeast for 2km to the tiny village of **Palauborrell**. ◄

From Palauborrell the landscape becomes distinctly coastal and very flat.

Turn south and then east along a dirt track and follow it for 2km to **Viladamat** (crossing a new road on the way into town).

Viladamat is a pretty town with bar and a restaurant and remnants of the original defensive walls.

278

From the roundabout on the eastern side of town follow the main road east for 800 metres. Turn left and head northeast and then east to a small settlement (Cinclaus), and continue east down to a road. Turn left and follow the road into **Sant Martí d'Empúries**.

The remains of the Greek city of Empúries

As well as the beautiful 'Bay of Roses' the walk ends with a historical gem, the remains of the Greek then Roman city of **Empúries**. The Greek city, which was originally located on an island at the mouth of the river Fluvià, was founded in the 6th century BC, developed as an important port and was the kick-off point for the Roman conquest of Spain. It chose the losing side in the war between Julius Caesar and Pompey, suffered a loss of status and declined in the face of competition from Tarragona.

Excavation didn't start until the beginning of the 20th century and is still ongoing but the foundations of the city centre have all been revealed. It's a

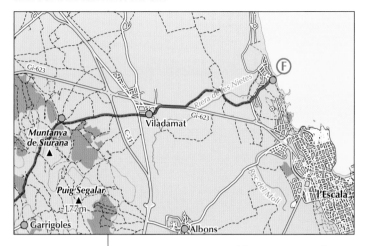

very interesting site, one of the most important of its
kind in Spain, and a timely reminder that the GR1 is
not just about medieval history.

APPENDIX A
Route summary tables

Summary of sections and stages

Section 1 – Puerto de Tarna to Reinosa

Stage		Distance (km)	Time	Ascent/Descent (m)	Page
Stage 1	Puerto de Tarna to Salamon	28	8-50	560/1040	39
Stage 2	Salamon to Prioro	19.5	7-20	1020/970	43
Stage 3	Prioro to Camporredondo de Alba	24.5	8-40	960/810	47
Stage 4	Camporredondo de Alba to Cervera de Pisuerga	30	9-20	680/900	51
Stage 5	Cervera de Pisuerga to Brañosera	33	11	1440/1240	56
Stage 6	Brañosera to Reinosa	24	7-40	530/890	62
Section totals		158.5	6 days	4950/5650	

Section 2 – Corconte to Berantevilla

Stage		Distance (km)	Time	Ascent/Descent (m)	Page
Stage 1	Corconte to Pedrosa de Valdeporres	23	7-30	550/700	69
Stage 2	Pedrosa de Valdeporres to Salazar	22.5	7-10	700/800	73

Stage	Distance (km)	Time	Ascent/Descent (m)	Page
Stage 3	Salazar to Paresot	31.5	9-50	640/610	77
Stage 4	Paresotas to Bóveda	23.5	7-30	630/630	82
Stage 5	Bóveda to Espejo	28	9-10	820/1010	86
Stage 6	Espejo to Fontecha	16	4-10	360/260	90
Stage 7	Fontecha to Berantevilla	30.5	9-30	710/750	93
Section totals		175	7 days	4410/4569	

Section 3 – Berantevilla to Olite

Stage	Distance (km)	Time	Ascent/Descent (m)	Page
Stage 1	Berantevilla to Peñacerrada	22	7-40	930/660	103
Stage 2	Peñacerrada to Bernedo	24	8-10	870/900	107
Stage 3	Bernedo to Santa Cruz de Campezo	19.5	6-15	510/580	111
Stage 4	Santa Cruz de Campezo to Los Arcos	29	10-00	1070/1250	114
Stage 5	Los Arcos to Larraga	39	10-40	300/350	118
Stage 6	Larraga to Olite	28	7-40	250/250	123
Section totals		161	6 days	4060/4130	

Section 4 – Olite to Murillo de Gállego

Stage		Distance (km)	Time	Ascent/Descent (m)	Page
Stage 1	Olite to Ujué	16	5-00	540/170	133
Stage 2	Ujué to Sos del Rey Católico	34	10-50	860/1010	136
Stage 3	Sos del Rey Católico to Petilla de Aragón	14	4-50	570/360	143
Stage 4	Petilla de Aragón to Biel	21	7-50	1010/1050	146
Stage 5	Biel to Murillo de Gállego	25	9-00	1030/1320	150
Section totals		110	5 days	4020/3860	

Section 5 – Murillo de Gállego to Graus

Stage		Distance (km)	Time	Ascent/Descent (m)	Page
Stage 1	Murillo de Gállego to Loarre	19	7-10	1320/1060	159
Stage 2	Loarre to Bolea	11	3-15	140/270	163
Stage 3	Bolea to Arguis	19.5	7-15	1050/700	166
Stage 4	Arguis to Nocito	19	7-10	1240/1360	170
Stage 5	Nocito to Paúles de Sarsa	36	12-00	1180/1260	174
Stage 6	Paúles de Sarsa to Ligüerre de Cinca	24.5	7-40	480/880	180
Stage 7	Ligüerre de Cinca to Tierrantona	16.5	6-30	950/770	184

Stage	Distance (km)	Time	Ascent/Descent (m)	Page
Stage 8	Tierrantona to Salinas de Trillo	16	5-30	690/560	187
Stage 9	Salinas de Trillo to Graus	26	9-00	900/1210	191
Section totals		187.5	9 days	7380/6970	

Section 6 – Graus to Gironella

Stage		Distance (km)	Time	Ascent/Descent (m)	Page
Stage 1	Graus to Lascuarre	21.5	6-30	520/580	199
Stage 2	Lascuarre to Puente de Montañana	33	11-00	1140/1160	202
Stage 3	Puente de Montañana to Àger	27	9-30	1040/980	208
Stage 4	Àger to Hostal Roig	31	11-20	1640/1160	213
Stage 5	Hostal Roig to Messanés	25.5	8-20	600/1080	218
Stage 6	Massanés to Oliana	26.5	8-30	690/890	222
Stage 7	Oliana to Cambrils	13.5	5-15	960/330	226
Stage 8	Cambrils to Sant Llorenç de Morunys	26	9-20	1090/1300	229
Stage 9	Sant Llorenç de Morunys to Sant Lleïr de la Vall d'Ora	24	9-00	1200/1290	232
Stage 10	Sant Lleïr de la Vall d'Ora to L'Espunyola	14.5	6-00	530/510	236
Stage 11	L'Espunyola to Gironella	20.5	5-30	660/310	240
Section totals		263.5	11 days	9680/9670	

Section 7 – From Gironella to the coast

Stage		Distance (km)	Time	Ascent/Descent (m)	Page
Stage 1	Gironella to Lluçà	30.5	9-00	710/440	247
Stage 2	Lluçà to Alpens	14	4-40	530/370	252
Stage 3	Alpens to Ripoll	21.5	7-40	860/1010	255
Stage 4	Ripoll to Sant Pau de Segúries	25	8-15	970/740	259
Stage 5	Sant Pau de Segúries to Oix	19.5	7-00	690/1130	263
Stage 6	Oix to Besalú	21	6-40	370/620	266
Stage 7	Besalú to Banyoles	14.5	4-10	250/290	270
Stage 8	Banyoles to Orriols	21	5-40	250/250	273
Stage 9	Orriols to Sant Martí d'Empúries	23	6-15	190/220	276
Section totals		191	9 days	4770/5090	
Route totals		1246.5km	53 days	39,270/39,930m	

Facilities along the way

Section 1 – Puerto de Tarna to Reinosa

Village/Town	Services (see legend)	Distance (km)	Cumulative distance (km)
Stage 1			
Puerto de Tarna	-	-	-
Marana	H S B	6	6
Salamon	H	22	28
Stage 2			
Las Salas	H R	3	31
Prioro	H R S	16.5	47.5
Stage 3			
Camporredonda de Alba	H R	24.5	72
Stage 4			
Ventanilla	R	22.5	94.5
Ruesga	H R B	5	99.5
Cervera de Pisuerga	H R B S ATM	2.5	102
Stage 5			
Arbejal	H	3	105
Barruelo de Santullán	H R	26	131
Brañosera	H R	3.5	134.5
Stage 6			
Reinosa	H R B S ATM	24	158.5

H = hotel/hostal/casa rural
R = restaurant
B = bar
S = shop
ATM = cashpoint

Section 2 – Corconte to Berantevilla

Village/Town	Services (see legend)	Distance (km)	Cumulative distance (km)
Stage 1			
Corconte	H R B	-	-
Ahedo de las Pueblas	B	13	13
Pedrosa de Valdeporres	H R B S ATM	10	23
Stage 2			
Nela	H	15.5	28.5
Salazar	H	7	35.5
Stage 3			
Torme	B	6.5	62
Paresotas	H	25	87
Stage 4			
Bóveda	H B R	23.5	110.5
Stage 5			
Valpuesta	R	14	124.5
Villanueva de Valdegovía	S B	3.5	128
Espejo	H R B S ATM	10.5	138.5
Stage 6			
Tuesta	H	2	140.5
Salinas de Anana	R	5	145.5
Fontecha	B	9	154.5
Stage 7			
Armiñón	R (?)	20	174.5
Berantevilla	R B	10.5	185

Section 3 – Berantevilla to Olite

Village/Town	Services (see legend)	Distance (km)	Cumulative distance (km)
Stage 1			
Berantevilla	R B	-	-
Peñacerrada	H R	22	22
Stage 2			
Bernedo	H R B ATM	24	46
Stage 3			
Maranón	B	6.5	52.5
Santa Cruz de Campezo	H R B S ATM	13	65.5
Stage 4			
Los Arcos	H R B S ATM	29	94.5
Stage 5			
Allo	R B S ATM	18.5	113
Larraga	H R B S ATM	20	133
Stage 6			
Berbinzana	B ATM	8	141
Olite	H R B S ATM	20	161

H = hotel/hostal/casa rural
R = restaurant
B = bar
S = shop
ATM = cashpoint

Section 4 – Olite to Murillo de Gállego

Village/Town	Services (see legend)	Distance (km)	Cumulative distance (km)
Stage 1			
Olite	H R B S ATM	-	-
Ujué	H R B	16	16
Stage 2			
Cáseda	R B S ATM	16	32
Sos del Rey Católico	H R B ATM	18	50
Stage 3			
Petilla de Aragón	H R B	14	64
Stage 4			
Biel	H R B	21	85
Stage 5			
Agüero	H R B	20	105
Murillo de Gállego	H R B	5	110

Section 5 – Murillo de Gállego to Graus

Village/Town	Services (see legend)	Distance (km)	Cumulative distance (km)
Stage 1			
Murillo de Gállego	H R B	-	-
Riglos	H R B	4	4
Loarre	H R B	15	19
Stage 2			
Bolea	H R B	11	30
Stage 3			
Arguis	H R B	19.5	49.5
Stage 4			
Nocito	H R B	19	68.5
Stage 5			
Paúles de Sarsa	H R	36	104.5
Stage 6			
Arcusa	H	3	107.5
Samitier	H	15	122.5
Ligüerre de Cinca	H R	6.5	129
Stage 7			
El Humo de Muro	H R	8.5	137.5
Tierrantona	H	8	145.5
Stage 8			
Salinas de Trillo	H	16	161.5
Stage 9			
Caneto	H	4	165.5
Graus	H R B S ATM	22	187.5

H = hotel/hostal/casa rural   S = shop
R = restaurant   ATM = cashpoint
B = bar

Section 6 – Graus to Gironella

Village/Town	Services (see legend)	Distance (km)	Cumulative distance (km)
Stage 1			
Graus	H R B S ATM	-	-
Capella	R	7.5	7.5
Lascuarre	H	14	21.5
Stage 2			
Puente de Montañana	H R B	33	54.5
Stage 3			
Corça	R	18	72.5
Àger	H R B ATM	9	81.5
Stage 4			
Hostal Roig		31	112.5
Stage 5			
Mecaners	H R	25.5	138
Stage 6			
Peremola	H R B S ATM	20	158
Oliana	H R B S ATM	6.5	164.5
Stage 7			
Cambrils	H R B	13.5	178
Stage 8			
Sant Llorenç de Morunys	H R B S ATM	26	204
Stage 9			
La Vall D'Ora	H R	24	228
Stage 10			
L'Espunyola		17	245
Stage 11			
Avivà	R B ATM	9	254
Gironella	H R B ATM	9	263

Section 7 – From Gironella to the coast

Village/Town	Services (see legend)	Distance (km)	Cumulative distance (km)
Stage 1			
Gironella	H R B ATM	-	-
Olvan	R B	4	4
Pont de Vilalta	R B	15.5	19.5
Llucà	H R	11	30.5
Stage 2			
Alpens	H R B S	14	44.5
Stage 3			
Ripoll	H R B S ATM	21.5	66
Stage 4			
Sant Joan de les Abadesses	H R B S ATM	14	80
Sant Pau de Segúries	H R B S ATM	11	91
Stage 5			
Oix	H R	19.5	110.5
Stage 6			
Tortellà	R B S ATM	12	122.5
Bansalú	H R B S ATM	9	131.5
Stage 7			
Banyoles		14.5	156
Stage 8			
Orriols	H	21	177
Stage 9			
Camållera	B R S	7	184
Viladamat	B R	12	196
Sant Marti di Empúries (L'Escala)	H R B S ATM	4	200

Views east from Coll de Comiols (Section 6, Stage 5)

APPENDIX B
A Spanish coast-to-coast

As well as combining great walking with history, the original designers of the GR1 wanted to set the challenge of a coast-to-coast walk – a walk that stretched across northern Spain and linked the Mediterranean with the Atlantic. Unfortunately the walking/climbing associations in Galicia and Asturias regions didn't get behind the vision and despite 'Finisterre' (on the Atlantic coast) being identified as the ultimate destination on waymarks in Castilla y León, the GR1 stops at Puerto de Tarna (at the regional boundary with the Asturias).

The lack of support from the Asturias in particular is perhaps understandable. The region, squeezed between the coast to the north and Cantabrian Mountains to the south, already has lots of east-west running routes, a number of which are pilgrim routes, and rather than creating another one it makes sense to link the GR1 to one of these.

If a coast-to-coast challenge is accepted than it is possible to take well-marked GR trails all the way from Finisterre to the Puerto de Tarna. Most of the routes are documented in the Cicerone Guide *The Northern Caminos* by Laura Perazzoli and Dave Whitson. Creating a coast-to-coast version of the GR1, utilising other routes, adds another 422km to the overall walk.

Starting at the Finisterre follow the Camino Finisterre east to Santiago de Compostela – this involves 84km of walking and can be completed in three days as follows.

• From Santiago de Compostela head east for 37km along the Camino del Norte to Arzua.
• From Arzua head east along the Camino Primitivo to Oviedo – eight days' walking and 205km.
• To get to the GR1 from Oviedo leave the Northern Caminos and join the GR105 the 'Ruta de las Peregrinaciònes' – another old pilgrim route that goes to Covadonga – which is the site of the battle that secured the Asturias for the Visigoths and Christianity.
• Head east along the GR105 for 50km (there is plenty of accommodation for the first 40km) to the Collada Llamosa where the GR105 meets the GR102, the 'Camin Real del Sallón'. Head south along the GR102 for 46km (Bezanes is a good place to stop for accommodation) and join the GR1 at Puerto de Tarna. Head east along the GR1 to the Mediterranean.

Spain is a very decentralised country and the availability and quality of information varies from region to region. Fortunately the access to information improves constantly as information aggregators like Google Maps, Trip Advisor and Booking.com extend their reach.

A forest trail approaching Pérex de Losa (Section 2, Stage 4)

APPENDIX C
Useful contacts

Walking Information

There is a national climbing and walking organisation with regional affiliated bodies. The regional bodies are responsible for the GR1 and other similar routes. Some provide 'topoguides' and GPX files for parts of the route on their websites.

National Federation
www.fedme.es

Castilla y León
www.fclm.com

The Basque Country
www.emf-fvm.com

Navarre
www.emf-fvm.com

Aragón
www.fam.es

Catalonia
www.feec.cat

Maps

The Spanish Mapping Agency – the Instituto Geográfico Nacional (www.ign.es) is responsible for the national mapping database and maintains maps at different scales including 1:25,000. These maps do not however consistently define the route of the GR1 and when they do the route described is not to be relied on. Paper maps can be bought from the Map Shop (www.themapshop.co.uk) and Stanfords (www.stanfords.co.uk).

Tourist Information

Tourist information in Spain is provided at many different levels – national, regional, provincial, urban – and for specific geographic areas, for example national parks. The national tourist board has an excellent website and included on it are links to all the tourist information offices around the country – see www.spain.info.

Although tourist information offices exist in many towns they usually have very restricted opening hours

All but the very smallest of villages will have a website where information about accommodation and other services can be found. A good way to find the website, and other local information on towns, is by using Wikipedia. Remember to use the Spanish (es-wikipedia.com) rather than the English version (en-wikipedia.com).

Booking.com is widely used by Spanish hotels and even casa rurals and some have even abandoned their websites in its favour. The intermediary is also a more reliable way of securing a reservation than an email. Google maps will also identify the location of nearly all the accommodation listed in this guide and provide contact details.

Transport

Public transport in Spain is comparatively good although finding out what's available can be a challenge. The bus/coach network, compared with the UK, is particularly extensive although unfortunately there is no single source of information.

Train

Renfe: www.renfe.com (including the narrow gauge services)

Bus

Movelia: www.movelia.es
Alsa: www.alsa.es
Alosa: www.alosa.es

Air

As well as Madrid, Oviedo (Asturias), Bilbao, Gerona, Barcelona and Zaragoza are all served by low-cost airlines.

Easyjet: www.easyjet.com
Ryanair: www.ryanair.com
Iberia: www.iberia.com
Vueling: www.vueling.com

Emergency and health

In the event of an emergency, help should be available in English on the European emergency number 112. If you're a UK resident remember to carry a European Health Insurance Card (EHIC) to secure free health care.

NOTES

NOTES

The Great Outdoors

DIGITAL EDITIONS
30-DAY FREE TRIAL

- Substantial savings on the newsstand price and print subscriptions
- Instant access wherever you are, even if you are offline
- Back issues at your fingertips

Downloading **The Great Outdoors** to your digital device is easy, just follow the steps below:

1 **Download the App** from the App Store

2 **Open the App**, click on 'subscriptions' and choose an annual subscription

3 **Download** the latest issue and enjoy

 Available on the App Store

The digital edition is also available on

The 30-day free trial is not available on Android or Pocketmags and is only available to new subscribers

 Available on Android **pocketmags**.com

LISTING OF CICERONE GUIDES

For full information on all our
guides, books and eBooks,
visit our website:
www.cicerone.co.uk.

Walking – Trekking – Mountaineering – Climbing – Cycling

Over 40 years, Cicerone have built up an outstanding collection of over 300 guides, inspiring all sorts of amazing adventures.

Every guide comes from extensive exploration and research by our expert authors, all with a passion for their subjects. They are frequently praised, endorsed and used by clubs, instructors and outdoor organisations.

All our titles can now be bought as **e-books**, **ePubs** and **Kindle** files and we also have an online magazine – **Cicerone Extra** – with features to help cyclists, climbers, walkers and trekkers choose their next adventure, at home or abroad.

Our website shows any **new information** we've had in since a book was published. Please do let us know if you find anything has changed, so that we can publish the latest details. On our **website** you'll also find great ideas and lots of detailed information about what's inside every guide and you can buy **individual routes** from many of them online.

It's easy to keep in touch with what's going on at Cicerone by getting our monthly **free e-newsletter**, which is full of offers, competitions, up-to-date information and topical articles. You can subscribe on our home page and also follow us on **Facebook** and **Twitter** or dip into our **blog**.

Cicerone – the very best guides for exploring the world.

CICERONE

2 Police Square Milnthorpe Cumbria LA7 7PY
Tel: 015395 62069 info@cicerone.co.uk
www.cicerone.co.uk and **www.cicerone-extra.com**